FOR
BREW
FRE
&BEA
GEEK

AKS
N
S...

Storm in a Teacup Coffeehouse | p66

*Indy Coffee Guide
Wales No.2*
is proudly sponsored by

Editor
Selena Young

Editorial team
Wiktoria Jazwinska
Abi Manning
Melissa Morris
Jane Rakison
Rosanna Rothery
Melissa Stewart

Editorial director
Jo Rees

Design
Tom Hampton
Dale Stiling

Community manager
Owen Penrice

Publishing
Charlotte Cummins
Tamsin Powell

Managing director
Nick Cooper

Cover image Coaltown Coffee Roasters

Big thanks to the *Indy Coffee Guide* committee (meet them on page 14) for their expertise and enthusiasm, and our partners Brew-It Group and Califia Farms.

Coffee shops, cafes and roasteries are invited to be included in the guide based on reaching criteria set by the committee, which includes using speciality beans, providing a high-quality coffee experience for visitors and being independently run.

For information on the *Indy Coffee Guides* visit

indycoffee.guide

indycoffeeguide

The right of Salt Media to be identified as the author of this work has been asserted by it in accordance with the Copyright, Designs and Patents Act 1988.

A catalogue record of the book is available from the British Library.

All rights reserved. No part of this publication may be reproduced, distributed, or transmitted in any form or by any means, including photocopying, recording, or other electronic or mechanical methods, without the prior written permission of the publisher, except in the case of brief quotations embodied in critical reviews and certain other non-commercial uses permitted by copyright law.

For permission requests, email Salt Media.

While every effort has been made to ensure the accuracy of the information in this publication, we cannot be held responsible for any errors or omissions and take no responsibility for the consequences of error or for any loss or damage suffered by users of any of the information published on any of these pages.

© Salt Media
Published by Salt Media, 2025
saltmedia.co.uk | 01271 859299
ideas@saltmedia.co.uk

ESPRESSO	3.2
MACCHIATO	3.4
CORTADO	3.4
AMERICANO / BATCH	3.4/5
FLAT WHITE	3.6
LATTE / CAPPUCCINO	3.8
MOCHA	4.2
HOT CHOCOLATE	3.8
CHAI LATTE	4.0
DIRTY CHAI	4.5
V60	4.6
ALT MILK 30P	SYRUP 50P

Contents

Page

12	Welcome
14	The team
18	Redefining speciality coffee
22	How to use the guide
25	Your adventures start here
	26 Maps
	28 South Wales
	82 Mid & West Wales
	112 North Wales
142	Notes
148	Index

WELCOME

There's no denying it: speciality coffee is having a big moment in Wales.

Since we published the first *Indy Coffee Guide Wales* in 2023 there's been an influx of exciting new coffee launches. This second edition of the guide – packed with 113 coffee shops, cafes and roasteries – showcases an even juicier bite of the cherry.

Buckle up for a rollercoaster ride of lip-smacking flavour thrills from independent cafes and roasteries. We've got you covered – from Cardiff to Carmarthen, and Llandudno to Llandeilo.

Rest assured there won't be any stomach-dropping lows on this ride, only euphoric caffeinated highs. That's because every *Indy Coffee Guide* member meets the strict criteria for inclusion. As a result, we're pretty confident that, with guide in hand, you'll never have a bad coffee again.

For us, one of the joys of visiting the venues is not knowing exactly what kind of experience we'll find. Food menus and coffee serve-styles change all the time, new bean-growing regions become popular, trends pop up, and fresh talent enters the field.

Some of the businesses in this guide have niche set-ups like vintage coffee wagons, while others focus their attention on particular foods (pie shops, doughnut stores and ice-cream parlours all feature).

What they all have in common is that they're independently run, deal in speciality coffee and deliver a top-notch experience.

We hope this guide becomes your passport to new coffee adventures. Use the new tick boxes at the top of the pages to keep track of the coffee shops you've visited and the roasteries' beans you've sampled.

Be sure to tag us in your caffeinated road trips and home brewing rituals; we love to find out where you've been and what you're drinking.

Selena Young
Editor

indycoffeeguide

The TEAM

Meet the crew who create the guides, and the Welsh coffee-industry experts who help decide who makes the grade to be included.

Editorial, production + design team

SALT MEDIA

This coffee-loving crew writes, proofreads, designs and manages each guide before releasing it into the wild through cafes, roasteries and bookshops. Their house-fave serve styles include V60 and french press, crafted with beans from local legends Roastworks and 51 Degrees North – plus coffees sent by roasteries across the UK (a nice perk of the job).

Scott James

COALTOWN COFFEE

Scott is the founder of the speciality roastery in Ammanford, Carmarthenshire. In 2019, Coaltown became the first speciality coffee roastery in the UK to earn B Corp certification, thanks, in part, to Scott's *'people before profit'* approach.

'We believe in bringing new industry to post-industrial towns across the UK. We started with our hometown and used coffee, a new "black gold", to fuel it,' says Scott. *'Sourcing from truly ethical producers and paying people properly make a positive difference at both ends of the supply chain.'*

Selena Young

SALT MEDIA

Editor of the *Indy Coffee Guides*, Selena keeps the brand vibe on-point. She writes coffee copy, reads and edits the writing team's work and goes out visiting cafes and roasteries. You'll often spot her at launch parties and coffee festivals – usually with a flat white in hand.

The TEAM

Owen Penrice

SALT MEDIA

You'll most likely come across Owen if you're a roastery or cafe owner; he's the key connector between the industry and the *Indy Coffee Guide* team. Before stepping into the role, Owen honed his palate and people skills as a barista, so he knows the daily grind inside out. Find him on Instagram @theindycoffeeguide_owen.

Steffan Huws

POBLADO COFFI

Steffan started Poblado Coffi in 2013, investing in a 5kg Toper which he installed in his shed. His roastery on the edge of Eryri National Park has grown steadily ever since, while staying true to its founding mission of being an ethical business.

'The quality of our produce is of equal importance to the relationships we develop with our customers, suppliers and the producers themselves,' says Steffan.

Sophie Smith

HARD LINES

Sophie launched Hard Lines in Cardiff with Matt Jones. What began in 2016 as a humble AeroPress bar has turned into one of the most popular coffee shops in the city, and a hugely successful roastery a few miles away. The team select, roast and serve speciality coffee that's been sourced sustainably with the aim of building relationships at origin.

'Hard Lines is a fun, energetic and creative coffee brand,' says Sophie. *'We challenge ourselves to do things differently and shake things up. Our goal is to build long-lasting relationships with producers and communities around the world.'*

Nick Cooper

SALT MEDIA

Nick founded Salt Media with Jo Rees in 2003 after becoming obsessed with speciality coffee while living in Sydney. Their plan to bring the (as then little-known) Aussie coffee vibes to the UK morphed into creating a food and drink publishing house – in which the *Indy Coffee Guide* now plays a starring role. Meet Nick at coffee festivals, launches and coffee industry events across the UK.

Farmer picking coffee cherries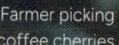

Redefining
SPECIALITY COFFEE

Every cafe and roastery in this guide deals in speciality coffee. But what exactly does 'speciality' mean, especially now the definition has been upgraded? Selena Young explains

What is speciality coffee?

There are two types of coffee grade: 'commodity' and 'speciality'. Commodity coffee is the bulk coffee traded on the financial markets, often harvested mechanically and roasted for mass consumption. It provides a less nuanced and, typically, inferior cup.

Speciality coffee, on the other hand, often comes from small farms and is cultivated in select altitudes and climates by farmers who nurture the crops with great attention to detail. Speciality coffee has long been defined by the Specialty Coffee Association (SCA) as coffee that scores 80 or above on a 100-point scale.

While commodity coffee has very few distinctive attributes, speciality coffee has many. The origin, producer, quality of coffee cherries, processing method and roasting are all important factors in how the final cup tastes.

Drying greens at origin

Making the grade

The role of assessing whether coffee falls into the commodity or speciality group – and where it sits on the 100-point scale – falls to a group of people called Q graders, who have expertise in identifying flavours and aromas.

Q graders use the SCA scale to identify beans as speciality grade, but the SCA has recently updated its grading system and amended its definition to emphasise that speciality coffee is: '*not solely determined by a score but by a holistic approach to value and includes sensory attributes, consistency, sustainability and the impact on the people who produce and enjoy it*'.

The new way of evaluating speciality is called the Coffee Value Assessment (CVA).

Coffee cupping

Coffee beans cooling after roasting

What is the CVA?

The CVA evaluates coffee via four separate assessments:

Physical – the coffee's green and roasted physical characteristics, including defect count, moisture content and bean size.

Descriptive – sensory analysis to document aroma, flavour, body, acidity and aftertaste.

Affective – consumer preference and perception, and capturing how different audiences experience and appreciate a coffee.

Extrinsic – factors beyond taste, such as variety, processing method, origin and sustainability practices.

Why change the framework?

The SCA has created the new assessment model to ensure a more inclusive, standardised and transparent evaluation of coffee quality and value across different contexts.

It also takes into consideration details that discerning coffee drinkers care about, such as whether the coffee is Fairtrade, produced by women or regeneratively grown.

From farm to flat white

Once green speciality beans arrive at roasteries in the UK, they're lightly roasted to preserve the specific characteristics that are the result of the terroir in which they were grown.

Roasters identify the flavours in the coffee they've roasted using a process called cupping. This involves slurping the brewed coffee off a spoon to identify its flavours. It's the same method employed by Q graders.

Speciality coffee beans are significantly more expensive to buy than commodity coffee, and they're treated with great care by baristas, who grind, brew and serve the beans in a way that respects the journey from origin to cup. The serve styles featured throughout this guide reflect that respect, as does the passion with which baristas and roasters talk about coffee.

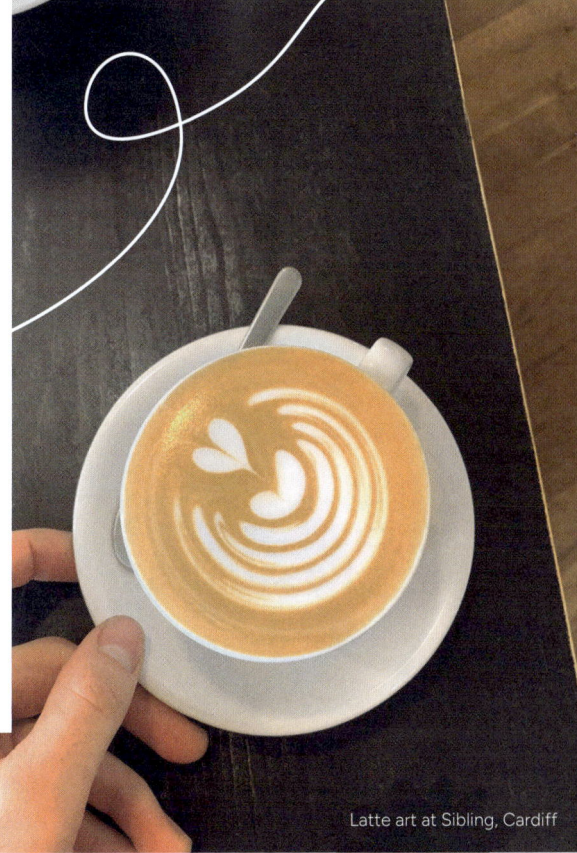

Latte art at Sibling, Cardiff

More good reasons to support speciality

By choosing to visit cafes that serve speciality beans, coffee fans are supporting coffee producers who are paid more for their crop and who, often, farm in more sustainable ways. The choice has a positive impact on the farming communities involved and helps build a more environmentally friendly coffee future for all.

How to use the GUIDE.

Coffee shops

The guide is split into areas to help you find speciality coffee spots to visit.

In each area, discover full-page and shot-size write-ups of coffee shops and cafes where you can slurp speciality brews.

Don't forget to tick the Been There symbol at the top of each page when you've visited a venue.

Roasteries

Meet leading speciality coffee roasters and discover where to source beans. Find them after the coffee shops in each area.

Use the Sipped That symbol at the top of each page to keep track of roasteries whose beans you've sampled.

Maps

Cafes and roasteries are numbered and marked on the map at the start of each section.

Follow us on Instagram ◉ indycoffeeguide

KEY

Symbols at the bottom of each cafe and roastery page provide further information on what you'll find at the venue.

Laptop friendly		Alcohol served	
Dogs welcome		Coffee courses	
Bike friendly		Roastery tours	
Reusable cup discount (Money off for bringing own cup)		Roastery tours (by appointment only)	
Outdoor seating		Buy beans in-store	
On-site coffee shop		Buy beans online	
Serving cakes + bakes		One of multiple sites	
Serving lunch + brunch		Welsh speaking	

Corner Coffee | p57

YOUR ADVEN- -TURES

START HERE

Maps

The guide is split into three sections, grouping together neighbouring areas to make it easier for you to find coffee shops and roasteries. Here's where each section starts.

28   South Wales

82   Mid & West Wales

112   North Wales

Mumbles Pier

Roasteries

54 Rate of Rise Coffee
55 Hard Lines
56 Welsh Coffee Co.
57 Kontext Coffee Company
58 Scout Coffee Roasters
59 Double Trouble Coffee Roasters

Locations are approximate

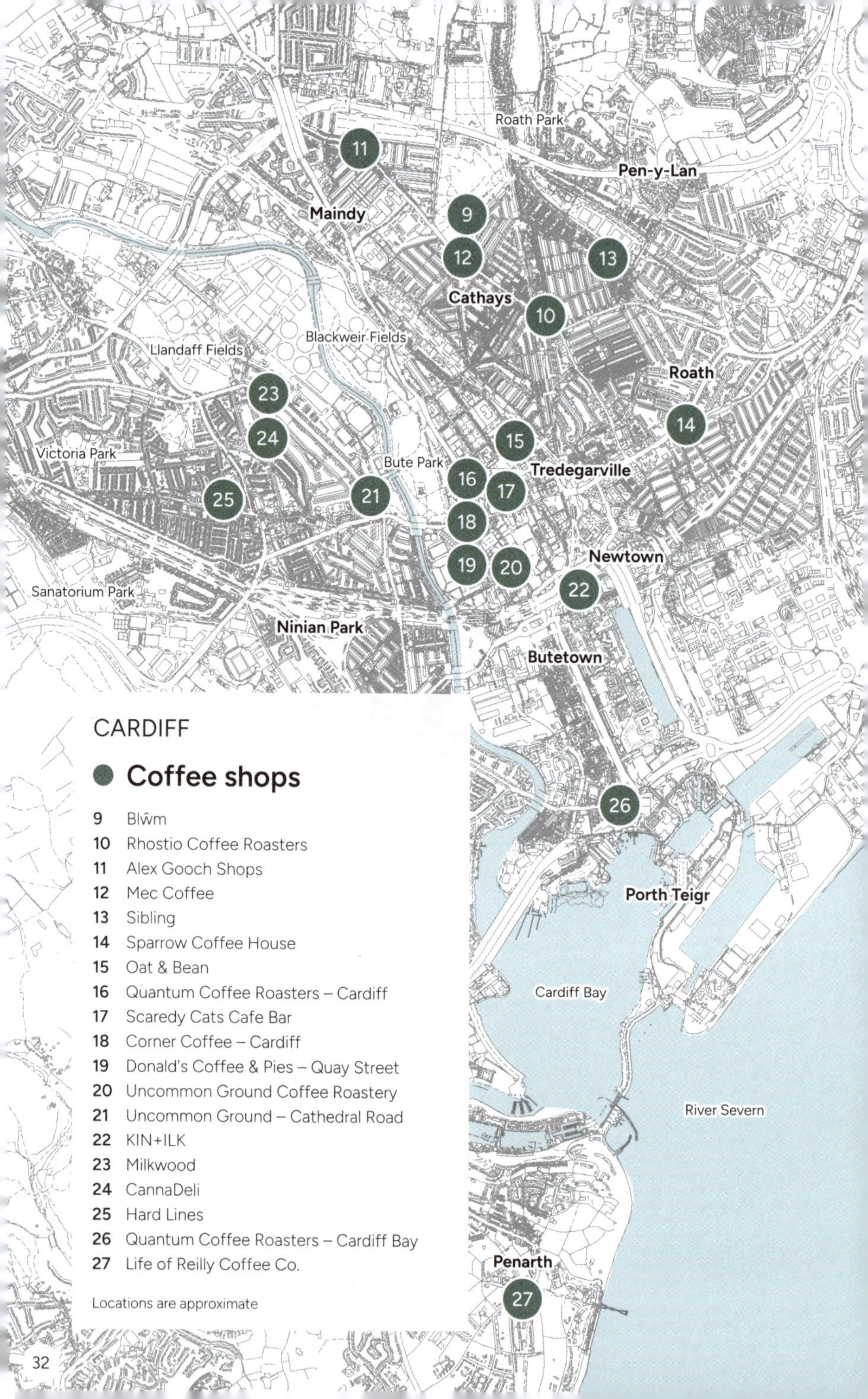

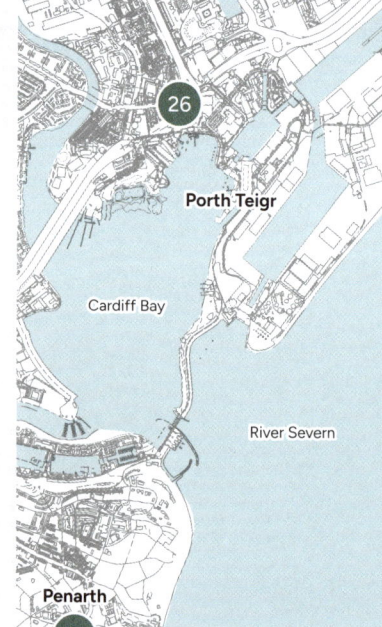

CARDIFF

● **Coffee shops**

9 Blŵm
10 Rhostio Coffee Roasters
11 Alex Gooch Shops
12 Mec Coffee
13 Sibling
14 Sparrow Coffee House
15 Oat & Bean
16 Quantum Coffee Roasters – Cardiff
17 Scaredy Cats Cafe Bar
18 Corner Coffee – Cardiff
19 Donald's Coffee & Pies – Quay Street
20 Uncommon Ground Coffee Roastery
21 Uncommon Ground – Cathedral Road
22 KIN+ILK
23 Milkwood
24 CannaDeli
25 Hard Lines
26 Quantum Coffee Roasters – Cardiff Bay
27 Life of Reilly Coffee Co.

Locations are approximate

Bean & Bread

36 Lion Street, Abergavenny, Monmouthshire, NP7 5PE
beanandbread.co.uk | 01873 778575
 beanandbread_

With its pretty Scandinavian-inspired design and collection of luscious houseplants, Bean & Bread delivers a calming, contemporary cafe experience in Abergavenny.

Inspired by her travels in New Zealand, owner Jessica Fletcher has created a space where bright interiors, warm hospitality and good coffee come together effortlessly.

The cafe has made its mark as a relaxed meeting spot for coffee lovers, brunch seekers and anyone needing a quiet place to catch up or unwind. Behind the bar, the team craft consistently excellent espresso using beans from Origin in Cornwall and rotating filters from guest roasteries. Whether you're after a lively espresso or smooth batch brew, the service is always friendly and unfussy.

ⓘ Grab a plant cutting from the wall to grow at home

The brunch menu leans into bold, bright flavours with tonnes of options for vegans and coeliacs. Standout dishes include keralan eggs with spiced yogurt, crispy onions and pomegranate, and the chilli fried eggs with labneh, focaccia, chilli butter and fresh herbs. It's the kind of fodder that surprises first-timers and makes regulars return for more.

Make tracks to the sister venue in Rogerstone, Newport, for brunches, good coffee and community vibes from Wednesday to Sunday.

Established
2018

Key roastery
Origin Coffee Roasters

Brewing method
Espresso, batch brew

Machine
La Marzocco Linea PB

Grinder
Mahlkonig E65S GBW

Opening hours
Mon-Sun
8.30am-4pm

The Dugout Cafébar

30 Lion Street, Abergavenny, Monmouthshire, NP7 5NT
dugoutcafebar.squarespace.com | 07475 815499
thedugoutcafebar

What was once a forgotten building off Abergavenny's main shopping area has been transformed into a homely forest-green den of perfectly poured coffees, craft pints and small-town soul.

It was born thanks to the vision of brothers Eoin and Will Duggan who, after building a business slinging flat whites from a converted horsebox, took on the neglected building. This involved gutting the inside, and the outside too.

A large garden at the back has been cleared and remodelled to create an unexpected oasis where visitors can sip coffee and drinks in the sun and engage with the live music, street food pop-ups and parties that dot the calendar. Further plans are afoot to expand the floor above and serve more food options.

Dig out your sneaks and sign up for Dugout's running club, Caffeine & Cardio

For now though, the indie cafe bar strikes the perfect balance between serving expertly dialled-in flat whites by morning, and cocktails and pints by night. Whenever you visit, local options are well repped – whether that's the bespoke house lager brewed in Crickhowell or the house coffee roasted in Blackwood by Eoin and Will's pals at Big Dog.

Established
2024

Key roastery
Big Dog Coffee

Brewing method
Espresso

Machine
La Spaziale S21

Grinder
Mahlkonig E65S GbW

Opening hours
Mon
9am–5pm
Tue-Wed
9am–6pm
Thu
9am–9pm
Fri-Sat
9am–10pm
Sun
9am–6pm
(seasonal opening hours)

Abergavenny

(3) The Angel Bakery

50 Cross Street, Abergavenny, Monmouthshire, NP7 5EU
theangelbakery.com | 01873 736950
angelbakeryabergavenny

The pretty market town of Abergavenny is a mecca for speciality coffee fans in this part of Wales as it's stacked with places to sink a decent brew. However, if you're looking for a flat white to-go, plus a tote bag stuffed with all manner of delicious baked goods, this should be your destination of choice.

The coffee in question is roasted by the exceptional Round Hill Roastery in Somerset and Cardiff's Hard Lines. Pair it with one of the exquisite cakes, biscuits and viennoiserie that line the generous counter. Unsure which to go for? The almond croissants and cinnamon swirls are firm favourites, but we particularly rate the organic-fruit-bejewelled danishes and cardamom sugarloaf brioche (named after nearby Sugar Loaf Mountain).

ⓘ This is a fave spot for walkers fuelling up for adventures in Bannau Brycheiniog National Park

All the luscious treats and loaves of chewy sourdough are handmade by the team (using flour from British mills) at their bakery just across the road.

Peruse the shelves stocked with branded merch, tote bags, coffee beans, Cardiff's Heist chocolate, Neal's Yard cheese and organic eggs, fruit and veg.

Established
2016

Key roastery
Hard Lines

Brewing method
Espresso, Moccamaster

Machine
Victoria Arduino Eagle One

Grinder
Victoria Arduino Mythos One

Opening hours
Tue-Thu
9am-4pm
Fri-Sat
8.30am-3.30pm

Baffle Haus

(4) Coffi Lab

'Lab' isn't a reference to uber-sterile coffee geekery but the joy of the humble labrador. Owner James' lab Dylan was the inspo for his career in coffee and this is repped in Coffi Lab's mission to raise money for Guide Dogs for the Blind. This Monmouth Lab is the original and one of a litter of ten.

80-82 Monnow Street, Monmouth, NP25 3EQ

coffilab.co.uk coffi.lab

(5) Baffle Haus

Motors, coffee and good eats collide at this pit stop. The cafe, part-owned by former rugby international George North, has been such a success for its bespoke Triple Co-roasted coffee and Baffle Brekkies it's spawned a sister site on the A48 near Cowbridge.

The Cedars, Goytre, Pontypool, NP4 0AD

bafflehaus.com bafflehaus

(6) Coffiology

The Roman baths and fort may be Caerleon's traditional points of interest, but speciality lovers head there to sip brews at this neighbourhood cafe. Locals and visitors squish in on sharing tables to drink Coaltown and Girls Who Grind coffee, scoff sausage rolls and slurp Joe's ice cream affogatos.

29 High Street, Caerleon, NP18 1AE

coffiology.com coffiology

⑦ Brickworks Coffee

Christchurch Centre, Malpas Road, Newport, Gwent, NP20 5PP
01633 822211
◉ brickworks.coffee

New-to-the-scene Brickworks Coffee has quickly amassed a fan following for what some are calling '*the best service station on the M4*'.

Just 30 seconds off Junction 26 of the M4, Brickworks is worth the hype, but is no roadside pit stop. With its design-led interior decor and relaxed atmos, it's more like an urban speciality venue than a motorway drive-through.

North Star espresso and Triple Co filter brews are served alongside a simple but satisfying brunch and lunch menu. Feast on old favourites like smashed avo on sourdough, french toast, and granola, or pair your pick of the coffee menu with a wedge of something sweet. The griddled chocolate and banana loaf from Carrot Top Bakery is reason enough to turn left off the inside lane.

🚴 On two wheels? Roll in straight off the road and leave your ride in the bike rack

Families love the kid-friendly play area, weekly toddler group and spacious layout, which includes a fully equipped Changing Places disability suite. Meanwhile, remote workers and pals catching up can usually find space on the long bench. Monthly board-game nights add a social twist, and a meeting room is available for motorway meet-ups.

Established
2024

Key roastery
North Star
Coffee Roasters

Brewing method
Espresso, batch filter, Kalita Wave

Machine
La Marzocco Linea PB

Grinder
Mahlkonig E65S GbW

Opening hours
Tue-Fri
8.30am-3pm
Sat
9am-2pm

⑧ Donald's Coffee & Pies – Radyr

Radyr Cricket Club, Station Road, Radyr, Cardiff, CF15 8AA

donaldspies.uk

📷 donalds.pies

Coffi & peis shouldn't be hard to translate even for those who don't speak Welsh. The tempting slogan is proudly emblazoned across Donald's vintage tawny-coloured Citroën HY coffee van, which takes up residency every summer at Radyr Cricket Club.

Whether you're watching or playing cricket at this spot on the bank of the River Taff, or a Cardiff caffeine fiend in search of sustenance, this is a find for homemade pies and banging brews.

⚡ Download Donald's digital loyalty card for delicious perks

Allpress is the house roastery, while filter coffees come courtesy of a roster of rotating roasteries including Hard Lines, Coborn, Skylark and Dark Arts. Like the coffee, pies are treated as an artform. Classics such as butter chicken, and beef, cheddar and onion gravy, are joined by limited-edition — and often themed — flavours.

A sister bricks-and-mortar site, located on Quay Street in the centre of Cardiff, provides the opportunity to sit in and explore the pie and coffee extravaganza in city surrounds.

Established
2024

Key roastery
Allpress Espresso

Brewing method
Espresso, filter

Machine
La Marzocco
Linea Mini

Grinder
Victoria Arduino
Mythos One

Opening hours
Sat-Sun
10am-4pm
(between April and September)

⑨ Blŵm

Fairoak House, Fairoak Road, Cardiff, CF24 4YA
blwmhome.co.uk
blwm_cardiff

There's a lot of loveliness to bask in at Blŵm. The lifestyle-store-meets-coffee-house is a feast for the senses, the kind of place you can savour a pretty tulip-topped flat white served from a ceramic cup, while perusing premium candles, coffee kit and homewares.

Ammanford's Coaltown supplies the freshly roasted beans, which are crafted into well-executed espresso drinks, batch brew and V60s by the pro baristas; the aroma of just-ground Coaltown coffee always foreshadowing the picture-perfect pours.

💧 Cardiff locals take note: Blŵm hosts a weekly run club and regular cocktail evenings

The team aren't afraid to flirt with drink trends and often shake up the menu to showcase seasonal specials such as rose-matcha latte, pistachio chai, and hot chocolate spiked with hazelnut and salted caramel.

Although freelancers visit to knuckle down to espresso-charged work in the space, Blŵm's calming aesthetic helps curate an atmosphere in which to slow down. After all, a single-origin pourover paired with a locally baked pastry shouldn't be rushed.

Established
2022

Key roastery
Coaltown Coffee Roasters

Brewing method
Espresso, V60, batch brew

Machine
La Marzocco Linea PB

Grinder
Mahlkonig E65S

Opening hours
Mon-Fri
8.30am-4.30pm
Sat-Sun
9am-4pm

⑩ Rhostio Coffee Roasters

16c Crwys Road, Cardiff, CF24 4NJ

rhostio.co.uk | 07463 942954

☐ rhostio_coffee

Overlooking Cardiff's buzzing cultural hub, this dynamic spot on Crwys Road is as lively as its surroundings. It's permanently busy with young professionals and students, who trade laptop tapping and daytime coffees for evening socialising and beers.

Floor-to-ceiling windows flood the roomy space with natural light and let daytime visitors bask in sunshine as they sip coffee made with Rhostio-roasted beans. Seasonal blend Cwtch is the house fave, or sample new blend Diana which delivers delicious notes of dark chocolate, brown sugar and caramel.

At sunset, the space transforms into a hotspot where DJs, musicians and comedians showcase their talents – both on the ground floor and a roof terrace with 360-degree city views.

◉ Unusually, bags of green beans are available in the retail section for those who want to give home-roasting a whirl

This community-focused spot is committed to giving everyone the opportunity to enjoy great coffee – both in the cafe and at home. Reusable coffee tins are available to buy and fill with discounted beans, and come with a free brew with each top-up, keeping customers consistently firing on all caffeinated cylinders.

Established
2021

Key roastery
Rhostio Coffee Roasters

Brewing method
Espresso, pourover, V60, AeroPress, batch filter

Machine
Faema E71

Grinder
Victoria Arduino Mythos One

Opening hours
Sun-Thu
10am-6pm
Fri-Sat
10am-10pm

(11) Alex Gooch Shops

While this bakery supplies some of the best cafes in the region with its doughy goods, its OG Whitchurch Road cafe is our fave place to snaffle lacquered pastries and sink well-made espresso.

45 Whitchurch Road, Cardiff, CF14 3JP

alexgoochbaker.com alexgoochbaker

(12) Mec Coffee

Since moving to Cathays from Castle Arcade, Mec has continued to bang the drum for quality speciality coffee, crafting brews using beans from the excellent Round Hill roastery and Skylark (plus guests). Brews are just half the story: natural wines complete the picture.

130 Crwys Road, Cardiff, CF24 4NR

 mec.coffee

(13) Sibling

This neighbourhood coffee bar and low-intervention bottle shop majors on the good things in life: coffee, carbs and quality wines. Swing by the cool caff – run by a sister and brother, of course – for delicious eats, pop-up events and, in good weather, to sip brews in the courtyard garden.

39 Lochaber Street, Cardiff, CF24 3LS

siblingcardiff.co.uk sibling_cardiff

(14) Sparrow Coffee House

Slow Saturdays are made for no-rush V60s sipped from a gorgeous ceramic cup in a cosy setting. Find exactly that, plus lush bakes, at Sparrow.

146 Clifton Street, Cardiff, CF24 1LZ

 sparrowcardiff

15 Oat & Bean

26 Park Place, Cardiff, CF10 3BA
oat.and.bean

This new plant-based addition to Cardiff's coffee scene has been a hit with more than just the vegan community; its speciality serves and easygoing groove have proved popular across the board.

Near the museum and university, yet tucked away from the main hubbub of the city centre, this a pleasing spot to take a caffeinated breather from the urban grind.

While Oat & Bean boasts plentiful seating, the best spots for people-watching while sipping a quality brew (with oat, coconut or soya milk) are at its large bi-fold windows. They're pulled back in summer for an inside-outside experience.

🍃 You have to rise early to get a cinny roll but each euphoric bite makes it worthwhile

Triple Co enjoys top billing as the house roastery (chosen because its beans pair perfectly with oat milk), while a wider range of roasteries enjoy guest roles on batch filter and cold brew. Roasteries are picked for more than simply bean quality and flavour; they're chosen because they have the same focus on sustainability and animal welfare as the O&B crew.

Cutting down on caffeine? The team make a mean matcha and churn lush smoothies – the mango and coconut is especially good. Food is, naturally, vegan and takes the form of stuffed croissants, topped toast, banana bread, granola, açaí bowls and delicious cakes and bakes.

Established
2024

Key roastery
Triple Co Roast

Brewing method
Espresso, batch filter, cold brew

Machine
Rocket RE Doppia

Grinder
Mahlkonig E65S GbW, Mahlkonig EK43

Opening hours
Mon-Thu
8am-5.30pm
Fri
8am-6pm
Sat
9am-6pm
Sun
9am-5.30pm

(16) **Quantum Coffee Roasters** – Cardiff

6-7 Duke Street, Cardiff, CF10 1AY

quantumroasters.co.uk | 07413 543335

quantumroasters

© Nikola Jurčáková

Situated opposite Cardiff Castle, Quantum's Duke Street outpost is a non-negotiable for anyone visiting the city's historic landmark. Since the cafe launched in 2023, it's become a go-to for visiting tourists as well as coffee geeks and those who enjoy working with a view (the front is entirely glazed).

Head inside to take in the vibrant decor, grab a freshly made toastie or savoury greek pastry and sip the signature Tiger Bay espresso while drinking in the sight of the towering castle. Alternatively, order to-go and take your brew for a walk through leafy Bute Park.

🍵 Go off-piste with the 100 per cent dark-chocolate mocha

Just like at Quantum's original Cardiff Bay location, the brews are crafted from own-roasted beans and shine in espresso drinks, pourovers and seasonal cold brew.

Each month, new sustainably sourced beans (often from small female-owned and small farms) are showcased, giving customers the opportunity to explore exciting flavour profiles from rare origins. Beans are also available to buy bagged for home use, alongside a newly expanded retail section of brew gear and mugs.

Established
2023

Key roastery
Quantum Coffee Roasters

Brewing method
Espresso, V60, cold brew

Machine
La Marzocco Linea

Grinder
Eureka Helios

Opening hours
Mon-Fri
9am-5pm
Sat
9am-6pm
Sun
10am-5pm
(seasonal opening hours)

(17) Scaredy Cats Cafe Bar

16 Working Street, St Davids Centre, Cardiff, CF10 1GN

scaredycatscafebar

Enthusiastic baristas, a massive range of beverages, top tunes, queer-friendly hospitality and an immaculate vibe are just a few of the reasons regulars rave about this pooch-friendly space in the city centre.

The coffee offering is pretty bang-on, too. The Scaredy Cats team have chosen Hundred House's chocolate-bomb CoCo blend for their house espresso and revel in its notes of dark choc and caramel wafer.

Things are switched up for cold and batch brew, and a rotating selection of guest beans highlight fun and funky flavours from roasteries across the UK. Coffees are best paired with the all-vegan cakes that crowd the counter, crafted by a local baker. Wacky and wonderful bakes and savoury snacks change weekly.

❂ Get stuck into the 100+ board games that are available for anyone to play

A collaborative spirit is woven through the fabric of Scaredy Cats and showcased in the seasonally curated drinks menu (created by the whole team), the vibrant mural in the bathrooms (painted by a team member), and in the merch (designed by another). There have been staff-led supper clubs too.

After dark, hit up Scaredy Cats for cocktails and craft beers from the likes of Lost and Grounded.

Established
2022

Key roastery
Hundred House Coffee

Brewing method
Espresso, batch brew, cold brew

Machine
La Marzocco Linea Classic

Grinder
Anfim SCODY II

Opening hours
Mon-Sun
9am-9pm

18 Corner Coffee – Cardiff

13 High Street, High Street Arcade, Cardiff, CF10 1AX

cornercoffee.uk

cornercoffee_co

Before even taking a sip of a Corner Coffee flat white you'll clock that you're in for a killer speciality experience. A neon-pink 'Brew Time' sign illuminates a bar adorned with high-spec coffee kit, while a huge retail selection features beans from some of the UK's most celebrated roasteries.

A team of young and talented baristas pull the shots, crafting on-point espresso drinks using beans from house roastery Triple Co Roast – plus a roundup of guests.

Just as impressive as the team's latte-art skills is the choice of filter coffees available: usually at least four are on hand to sample as V60, batch or AeroPress, and there are plans to expand the menu even further.

The crew's favourite roasteries often visit to host cuppings and menu takeovers

All this makes Corner Coffee a magnet on the High Street for creatives and coffee-loving folk. Conversation between punters flows as smoothly as the pours and helps create a good vibe.

Stick around for longer than it takes to get a quick caffeine fix, because the brunch dishes are delish (and usually involve slabs of squeaky halloumi).

Established
2017

Key roastery
Triple Co Roast

Brewing method
Espresso, batch brew, V60, AeroPress

Machine
Victoria Arduino Eagle One

Grinder
Mahlkonig E80, Mahlkonig E65S GbW

Opening hours
Mon-Fri
8.30am-5pm
Sat-Sun
9am-5pm

19 Donald's Coffee & Pies – Quay Street

18-19 Quay Street, Cardiff, CF10 1EA

donaldspies.uk

donalds.pies

If you see a queue curling around the entrance of an eatery on Quay Street, chances are it will be espresso enthusiasts seeking out Donald's for its quality brews and comforting homecooked pies.

The brand was founded by Donald's grandson Gareth, who first gave Cardiff a taste of the unbeatable combo of gourmet coffee and pies from his van, which he parked up on the weekend at Riverside Ground in Radyr (it's still there to this day).

♥ Rep Donald's quirky cartoon branding in the range of merch

Then, in 2024, Gareth launched this tiny bricks-and-mortar site near the Millenium Stadium which, with its retro-caff exterior, diner-style decor and buzzy vibe has been a big hit.

Coffee is crafted from house roastery Allpress beans, while an ever-changing line-up of roasting royalty – including Hard Lines, Coborn, Skylark and Dark Arts – provides guest filter options.

The pie array is just as enticing, featuring a range of classics as well as rotating specials. If you can't decide which to go for, the traditional JC (stuffed with mince, onion gravy and vintage cheddar) is a fan favourite for good reason.

Established
2024

Key roastery
Allpress Espresso

Brewing method
Espresso, filter

Machine
La Marzocco Linea PB

Grinder
Victoria Arduino Mythos One

Opening hours
Mon-Fri
8am-4pm
Sat-Sun
9am-4pm

(20) Uncommon Ground Coffee Roastery

10-12 Royal Arcade, Cardiff, CF10 1AE
uncommon-ground.co.uk | 07495 504014
_uncommonground

In 2025, Uncommon Ground celebrate ten years of slinging espresso, brewing pourovers and stacking avo toast at their flagship site.

The OG coffee shop (the Welsh capital's oldest roastery-cafe) is tucked away in one of Cardiff's historic arcades and offers plenty of spots where customers can sip the good stuff while watching the world go by.

Over the years, the team have perfected their signature house espresso: a blend of Brazilian, Colombian and Indonesian beans that delivers notes of plum, toffee and chocolate orange. Follow your nose and the sweet toasty aroma of coffee will guide you right to this nook in the heart of the city.

🞄 Get a second bite of the coffee cherry at the sister shop in Pontcanna

The space is especially busy on weekends when customers make a beeline for brunch and a juicy batch brew. Arrive early if you want to sit in while sinking your teeth into the ever-popular breakfast burrito and slurping a dynamite brew.

Game to branch out from your usual order? Ask the barista what's brewing in the Tone Swiss – there aren't many spots in the city housing one of these swish brew machines.

Established
2015

Key roastery
Uncommon Ground

Brewing method
Espresso, V60, drip, cold brew

Machine
La Marzocco Linea PB

Grinder
Mahlkonig EK43,
Mahlkonig E80S,
Compak E8,
Anfim Pratica

Opening hours
Mon-Fri
8.30am–5pm
Sat
9am–5pm
Sun
10am–5pm

21 **Uncommon Ground** – Cathedral Road

5 Avalon House, 7 Cathedral Road, Cardiff, CF11 9HA

uncommon-ground.co.uk

_uncommonground

When the Uncommon Ground tribe unlocked the doors to their second Cardiff site, they gave the people of Pontcanna what they'd been yearning for: another spot in the city to source uncommonly good brews.

Like the Royal Arcade original, this Cathedral Road outpost deals in uber-fresh beans which are roasted by the team and regularly switched up. The result is a seasonal rotation of delicious coffees brewed by trained baristas to highlight unique flavour profiles.

💡 Spread the coffee love: treat a pal to a bag of fresh UG beans from the retail shelf

The house espresso is always a lip-smacking safe-bet coffee, but a range of single origins can be found on batch brew for more unexpected flavour thrills.

While this spot has less of a brunch focus than Royal Arcade, the food is above-par and leans into convenient bites for nearby office workers and residents. Freshly made baguettes and savoury pastries are always up for grabs and go down a treat with a silky flat white.

Established
2023

Key roastery
Uncommon Ground

Brewing method
Espresso, drip,
cold brew, batch brew

Machine
La Marzocco
Linea Classic S

Grinder
Anfim Pratica

Opening hours
Mon-Fri
7.30am-4pm
Sat-Sun
9am-4pm

CannaDeli

22 KIN+ILK

There are five members of the Kin+Ilk family spread across the city. However, it's impossible to pick a fave sibling as each spot guarantees flavour-forward coffees and next-gen cafe bites in cool contemporary surrounds.

1 Capital Quarter (Smart Way), Tyndall Street, Cardiff, CF10 4BZ

kinandilk.com kinandilk

23 Milkwood

Good food calls for good coffee, and the high-status brunch dishes (hello buttermilk-fried-chicken waffles) at this cafe-restaurant go down a treat with Clifton Coffee-fuelled flat whites.

83 Pontcanna Street, Cardiff, CF11 9HS

milkwoodcardiff.com milkwoodcdf

24 CannaDeli

Feast on trad rarebit or jammy eggs with smashed avo and salmon on rye, then wash it down with Poblado espresso at this hidden indie off Kings Road.

Unit 2 Pontcanna Mews, 200 Kings Road, Cardiff, CF11 9DF

cannadeli.co.uk cannadeli

25 Hard Lines

Diner-style seating, a tonne of homemade eats and own-roasted coffee are just a few of the attractions on offer at Hard Lines' cafe HQ. Arrive early on weekends as the queue is usually halfway down the road by brunchtime. Taking home merch featuring the brand's cheery mug man is a must-do.

Canton, Cardiff, CF5 1GX

hard-lines.co.uk hardlinescoffee

26 **Quantum Coffee Roasters** – Cardiff Bay

58 Bute Street, Cardiff, CF10 5BN
quantumroasters.co.uk | 07413 543335
quantumroasters

© Nikola Jurčáková

It's not easy sourcing unique coffees that are hands-down delicious from responsibly sustainable sources – including many female producers – but that's exactly what Quantum delivers.

Using beans from its own roastery in the city, Quantum specialises in serving rare coffees sourced from the likes of Hawaii, Galapagos and Jamaica, as well as beans from female-led farms in Rwanda, Honduras and beyond.

Those looking to experience flavour fireworks should make a beeline for the original site on Cardiff Bay or the new sister site opposite the castle on Duke Street. Both deliver sterling brews and vibrant colour – there's not a whiff of Nordic minimalism at Quantum.

🛈 Check out Wales-inspired Gwalia, a bespoke blend delivering caramel, cocoa, orange and nutty notes

Typically, two new coffees are introduced each month and launched via a limited-edition spot on the brew bar. Customers are encouraged to sample the single origins as filter and to try the signature Tiger Bay blend in espresso drinks.

As well as gaining a following for its constantly evolving catalogue of coffees, Quantum has made a name for itself as a destination for summer refreshment: it's got nitro cold brew on tap.

Established
2015

Key roastery
Quantum Coffee Roasters

Brewing method
Espresso, V60, nitro cold brew, cold brew

Machine
La Marzocco Linea

Grinder
Eureka Helios

Opening hours
Mon-Fri
8am-5pm
Sat
9am-5pm
Sun
10am-5pm
(seasonal opening hours)

NEVER HAVE A BAD COFFEE AGAIN

Guides also available for **London**; **The South**; **North, Midlands & East**; and **Scotland**. Shop the full range and merch at

indycoffee.guide

☉ indycoffeeguide

27 Life of Reilly Coffee Co.

Off Edge, Station Approach, Penarth, Vale of Glamorgan, CF64 3EE

lifeofreillycoffee.co.uk

lifeofreillycoffee

It may be a teeny tiny coffee shop – just 1.5m x 2m – which operates out of a converted broom cupboard, but Life of Reilly punches way above its weight.

Located in a Victorian building next to Station Approach in Penarth, the coffee hatch is a favourite with commuters who are delighted to score a speciality-grade brew for their daily train journey.

Founder Liam Reilly opened the space in 2024. However, he already had form serving good brews to discerning drinkers via a coffee van (a Volkswagen he converted with his grandad). In fact, he still takes it to sling espresso at events, festivals and film sets.

Planning a party? Make sure everyone's well caffeinated by hiring the Life of Reilly coffee van

Despite this new outlet's bijou size, customers often tell Liam they feel they're getting the full cafe experience from the hatch due to his kind and knowledgeable service. It's complemented by fresh pastries from Tŷ Melin Bakery, high-spec coffee equipment (which takes up every inch of counter space) and the use of flavourful beans.

Triple Co Roast provides the house coffee – two espresso options, as well as a filter that changes weekly – and there are plans afoot to bring in a rotation of guest coffees. Watch this space.

Established
2024

Key roastery
Triple Co Roast

Brewing method
Espresso, batch brew, cold brew

Machine
La Marzocco Linea PB, Victoria Arduino Eagle One Prima

Grinder
Mahlkonig EK43 S, Victoria Arduino Mythos One

Opening hours
Mon-Fri
6am-2pm
Sat
8am-1pm

(28) Stomping Ground

Llantwit Major train station, Le Pouliguen Way,
Llantwit Major, Vale of Glamorgan, CF61 1AF

07875 758266 | stomping_ground_coffee

Like something out of a Wes Anderson film, this converted 1979 Renault Estafette (first name Gloria, last name "Estevan") delivers a dose of nostalgia with its colourful palette of orange and pink.

The retro style is complemented by the picturesque latte art crafted by owner Lucy Payne, while a waggy welcome comes courtesy of her golden lab Howie. The vintage coffee wagon, which parks up at Llantwit Major train station, is so engaging it attracts a range of regulars including commuters, dog walkers, parents on the school run and coffee fans.

☕ Sweltering heat? Cool off with an iced latte or matcha

Beans are sourced from Hard Lines – and not just because the roastery's creative coffee bags and merch look great in this setting. The espresso is reliably delicious whether served straight-up from the Fracino or with glossy steamed milk.

The coffee is complemented by a stock of locally made bakes from Llys Y Garn Bakery (try the cult-status millionaire's shortbread) and a fridge packed with pots of homemade granola.

Outdoor seating, nearby bike racks, treats for dogs and free babyccinos for sprogs are thoughtful touches that have helped make this a community fave.

Established
2020

Key roastery
Hard Lines

Brewing method
Espresso

Machine
Fracino Contempo

Grinder
Anfim Lunar

Opening hours
Mon-Fri
7.30am-12.30pm
Sat
(Occasional - keep an eye on social)

㉙ Welsh Coffee Co.

Community Hall, Slon Lane, Ogmore-by-Sea, Vale of Glamorgan, CF32 0PN
welshcoffee.com
welshcoffeeco

This outpost of the established Ewenny roastery is an eco-friendly coffee shop that serves award-winning brews and community vibes in equal measure. The cafe in Ogmore's new community hall is a determinedly inclusive space for all.

Founder Huw Williams established Welsh Coffee Co. in 2011 and his passion for the great outdoors has been at the heart of the business since day one. Making the connection to nature has seen Huw and team instigate sustainable solutions such as using solar-generated electricity and flame-roasting beans.

🚴 Bikes can be locked up at the new racks while their owners enjoy a caffeinated pit stop

The roastery is a Great Taste award winner, having bagged two stars for its Mor, Nicaragua and Bendigedig coffees, and a star for the Aur/Gold – the beans used for espresso in the cafe. This washed and sun-dried medium roast is a blend of quality arabica (bourbon and caturra) beans from Nicaragua and Panama. In the cup it's deliciously well balanced with choc-caramel-apricot notes and a smooth finish.

Grab a coffee to-go and explore the nearby coast or sit in and enjoy the cafe's sea views as you sip.

Established
2023

Key roastery
Welsh Coffee Co.

Brewing method
Espresso

Machine
La Marzocco Strada

Grinder
Mahlkonig

Opening hours
Mon-Fri
9am-4pm
Sat-Sun
9am-5pm

Corner Coffee – Porthcawl

16 Jennings Building, The Harbour, Porthcawl, Bridgend, CF36 3XA

cornercoffee.uk

cornercoffee_co

Seven years after launching Corner Coffee on Cardiff's High Street, the gang took their sterling coffee offering to the seaside and opened this swish coffee and brunch spot on Porthcawl's harbour.

This new sibling offers the same quality coffee and food as its big brother in the city, but pairs them with sea views and a more tranquil atmosphere.

Take your time deciding what to blow your caffeine allowance on as the menu is vast and designed to cater to all palates – from fussy to the-funkier-the-better. The house espresso is roasted by Triple Co Roast in Bristol and is supplemented by guest beans for filter from the likes of Curve, Skylark, OddKin and Radical.

🔵 Warm up post-surf with a brew and a breakfast bap

Corner's filter offering is unrivalled in the town, so we'd recommend plumping for a fruity V60. If you like it, you can pick up the beans – and even pourover equipment – from the retail shelves to recreate the experience in your own kitchen.

Even on chilly days, there's pleasure to be found in watching the waves roll in while sipping a flat white and munching a pastry while seated on one of the outdoor benches. However, stylish interiors and cosy seating areas make breakfast, brunch or lunch inside a lovely experience, whatever the weather.

Established
2024

Key roastery
Triple Co Roast

Brewing method
Espresso, batch brew, V60

Machine
Rocket RE Doppia

Grinder
Mahlkonig E80, Mahlkonig E65S GbW

Opening hours
Mon-Sat
8am-5pm
Sun
9am-5pm

Beat Bakehouse

1a Station Hill, Bridgend, CF31 1EA

beatbakehouse.com

@ beatbakehouse

Bridgend's commuters have it pretty cushy with a cafe-bakery-coffee-shop of this quality right by the train station – every working day can start off on the right foot. The set-up by wife-and-husband team Hollie and Adrian Moses offers a sweet combo of locally roasted speciality coffee, house bakes and Nordic interiors.

While the house coffee (Coaltown's velvety Black Gold blend) is delicious, the just-baked breads, pastries and cakes are also first class. From fully loaded seasonal sourdough focaccia sandwiches and giant sausage rolls to blueberry and lemon bundt cake, it's all good. The extensive food offering regularly features vegan treats too – time your visit right and you could bag a squidgy plant-based cinnamon knot.

Beat's bakers like to keep returning customers on their toes with a seasonally changing croissant: the twice-baked, triple-cheese welsh rarebit with sautéed leek, whipped feta and crisp cheese shards still lives rent-free in the minds of the regulars.

Peruse the revamped retail section stocking Ozone and Dark Arts coffee beans

While most pair their carby contraband with a Black Gold 'spro, there's always a guest espresso available, as well as a monthly changing single-origin batch brew sourced from guest roasteries like Hard Lines, Ozone and Clifton.

Established
2022

Key roastery
Coaltown Coffee Roastery

Brewing method
Espresso, batch brew

Machine
La Marzocco Linea PB ABV

Grinder
Mahlkonig EK43, Mahlkonig E65S GbW

Opening hours
Mon-Fri
6.30am-3pm
Sat
8am-1pm

Whocult Coffee + Donuts

Unit 1d Kingsway Buildings, Bridgend Industrial Estate, Bridgend, CF31 3YH
whocult.com | 01656 648537
whocult

Obsessed with the cult-classic pairing of coffee and donuts? Then this cafe bakery with six outlets in South Wales is going to be your jam.

Whocult stands out from the crowd as a result of its outrageous doughy creations, speciality brews that thrum with flavour, and punchy identity (check out sister streetwear brand Whoclo).

Every donut is made from scratch at this bakery HQ in Bridgend and delivered fresh each morning to sites in Porthcawl, Cardiff, Barry, Newport and Swansea. For a visual taste of the team's creative confections, check out Whocult's website and socials which showcase house faves like Biscoff, Bueno, Reese's and Homer chocolate, plus seasonal and wildcard limited editions such as lemon meringue pie, millionaire's shortbread and praline profiterole.

⏰ Special occasion coming up? Order a box of customised donuts

Visitors' carby fantasies are suitably matched with caffeine thrills. The house coffee, a bespoke El Salvadoran blend from Welsh Coffee Co., is crafted with care and creates a pleasing counterbalance to the donuts' sweetness thanks to its nutty, bold flavour.

Established
2019

Key roastery
Welsh Coffee Co.

Brewing method
Espresso, filter

Machine
La Marzocco
Linea Classic S

Grinder
Mahlkonig E80

Opening hours
Mon-Sat
10am-6pm
Sun
10am-4pm

(33) The Hyde Out

Kenfig Nature Reserve, Ton Kenfig, Bridgend, CF33 4PT

doubletroublecoffee.co.uk

thehydeoutcoffee

The Hyde Out's humble beginnings (serving espresso from a horsebox) paved the way for its current set-up as a coffee and food hatch at Kenfig Nature Reserve.

In this picturesque location, the team create speciality brews using beans from sister roastery Double Trouble Coffee, which are slurped either undercover at the adjoining seating area or from one of the outdoor benches. It's an unbeatable way to get a coffee fix while soaking up the calm of the natural surroundings.

The own-roasted beans guarantee luscious espresso drinks, but for fruity thrills try one of the single origins as drip or batch — the baristas favour Ethiopian beans for their juicy flavours.

⚡ Pick up a bag of Double Trouble Coffee for your home hopper

Whether you're arriving rosy-cheeked and famished after a long walk through the reserve, or powering up before your adventures, carb load with a chunky slab of local cake from the groaning countertop. Savoury fodder can also be found in bagels, paninis, scotch eggs and sausage rolls.

Before launching The Hyde Out, founder Emma Hyde worked in costume design for film and TV, so it's fitting she's also launched an outpost at Dragon Studios near Pencoed.

Established
2020

Key roastery
Double Trouble Coffee

Brewing method
Espresso, filter

Machine
Fracino Contempo

Grinder
Eureka

Opening hours
Mon-Sun
10am-4pm
(seasonal opening hours)

34 Clwb Coffi

121 Dunraven Street, Tonypandy, Rhondda Cynon Taff, CF40 1AS
clwbcoffi.com | 01443 307110
clwbcoffi

© Shan

Forget the Groucho Marx quip about refusing to join any club that would have you as a member: this Tonypandy coffee shop is a clwb that's open to everyone and yet is a delight to be a part of.

That's not just because of its expertly poured speciality brews made with Origin beans, or the result of a banging brunch menu boasting the likes of smoky beans on toast with feta and spring onions, and bouncy pancake stacks. It's not even due to the welsh cakes done three ways (chocolate, trad and with jam). It's because of the vibe.

ⓘ Check out the open-mic nights, quiz evenings and more

This is a community coffee shop in the truest sense of the word, acting as a beacon on Tonypandy's high street. It's brought a sense of rejuvenation that's been badly needed and become a focal point where locals with an appreciation of good coffee can congregate. Parents with pushchairs, young professionals, retired couples and every other demographic in between fill the cafe with chat and the clink of cutlery on plates.

The good vibes are fuelled by owners John and Sarah who, with their cheerful team, have created something super special at Clwb Coffi. On our visit we left having had hugs with strangers and welsh cakes bought for us by new friends. Extraordinary.

Established
2020

Key roastery
Origin Coffee Roasters

Brewing method
Espresso, batch brew

Machine
La Marzocco Linea PB

Grinder
Mahlkonig EK43, Victoria Arduino Mythos One

Opening hours
Mon-Fri
8.30am-4pm
Sat-Sun
9am-3pm

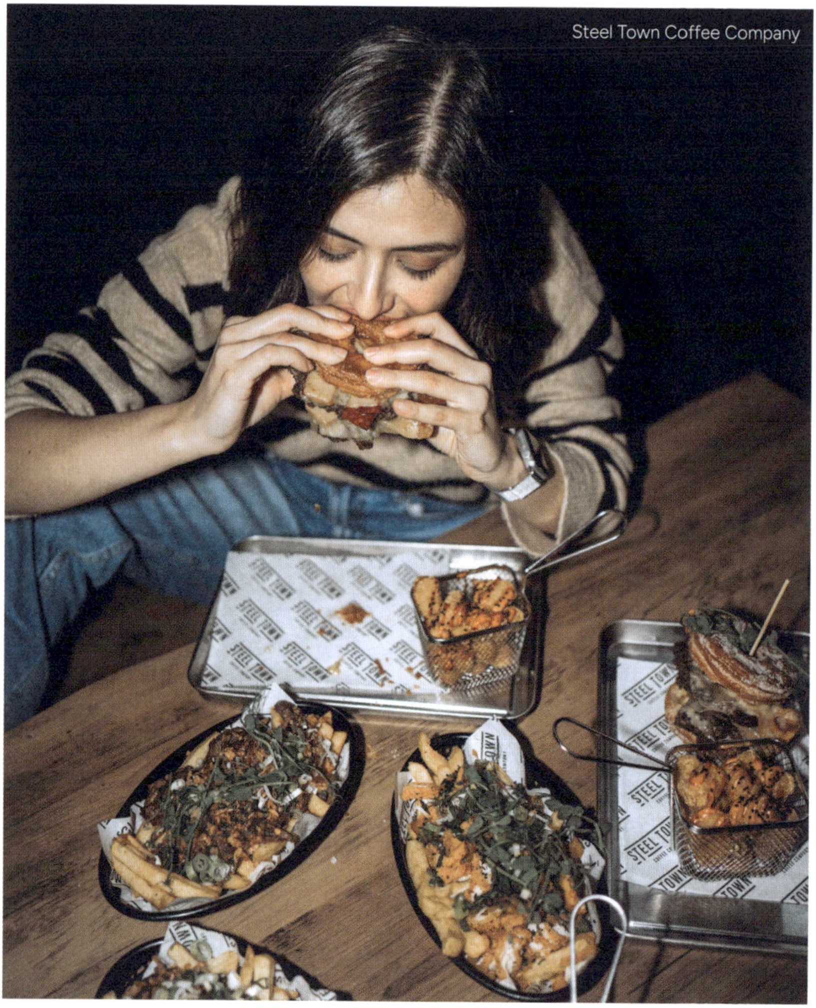

Steel Town Coffee Company

35 Haystack Cafe – Merthyr Tydfil

Haystack's cafes are always lively hubs in their communities – there's another in Swansea and a flagship cafe about to launch in Cardiff – and this is no exception. Visit for Coaltown brews, a great selection of eats and a good-times vibe.

39 High Street, Merthyr Tydfil, CF47 8DE

haystackcafeorder.com haystackcafe

36 Steel Town Coffee Company

Port Talbot's neighbourhood cafe offers more than just quality speciality coffee: it's the place to chow down on 'Sick Hot Chick Burgers' and 'What is It With The Welsh and Curry Sauce Loaded Fries'. The only obstacle to a good time is feeling a bit twp saying that out loud when you order.

280 Margam Road, Port Talbot, SA13 2DB

steeltowncoffeeco

Booths by the Bridge

Dulais Fach Road, Tonna, Neath, SA10 8EP
boothsbythebridge.co.uk | 07582 940220
boothsbythebridge

A carefully curated interior and gorgeous views (the River Neath flows just beyond Booths' spacious garden, and a historic aqueduct can be spotted in the distance) make this a find for unhurried caffeination.

Inside, natural stone walls, an oak bar and flagstone floors create a cottagecore vibe that's complemented by local artist David Williams' impressionist paintings of the surrounding landscape. Outside, a leafy riverside garden is the place to sink a brew on sunny days.

In winter, cosy up with a well-crafted coffee next to the large open fire

Although the Booths team are pretty new to the cafe game, they've won the hearts of local coffee lovers by serving high-grade beans from Coaltown crafted into top-notch espresso drinks.

Freshly baked pastries, cakes and baguettes make a fine accompaniment to the coffees, and the team are developing the food offering further to keep showcasing quality local ingredients. Keep 'em peeled for Disco Dough pop-ups in the garden – afternoons by the river are that bit more delicious with Neapolitan-style pizzas.

In the afternoons, brews are supported by a line-up of Welsh spirits, local wines and refreshing lagers.

Established
2025

Key roastery
Coaltown Coffee Roasters

Brewing method
Espresso

Machine
La Marzocco Linea Classic S

Grinder
Mahlkonig E65S GbW

Opening hours
Mon, Thu, Sun
9am-4pm
Fri-Sat
9am-8pm

38 Monty's

Unit 5 Shufflebotham Lane, Neath, SA11 3FJ
07471 087423
montyscoffeeneath

Monty's continues to go from strength to strength since it switched up its offering from mobile van to bricks-and-mortar coffee shop in 2022.

A recent upgrade to the coffee offering has been Monty's own luscious house blend – a result of a longterm partnership with Coaltown – which has proved a huge hit with returning and new customers alike. The team have also made connections with speciality roasteries of note from across the globe, leading to a diverse brew menu that delights coffee enthusiasts while also setting the cafe apart from others nearby.

Word on the street is that Monty's may open more coffee shops. Watch this space ...

Guest roasteries including The Barn in Germany, Ireland's 3FE, Bluebird Coffee in South Africa and Spain's Nomad have each graced the hopper of the Mahlkonig grinders. The lush guest beans are also featured for a limited time on the retail shelf so customers can continue the flavour thrills at home.

The consistently bang-on pours can be paired with freshly baked pastries – savoury and sweet – supplied by Monty's pals at Pitchfork & Provision in Llandeilo, as well as healthy grab-and-go options from Athlete Kitchen in Pontyclun.

Established
2020

Key roastery
Coaltown Coffee Roasters

Brewing method
Espresso, batch filter

Machine
La Marzocco Linea Classic S

Grinder
Mahlkonig E65S GbW × 3

Opening hours
Mon-Fri
7am-4pm
Sat
8am-3pm
Sun
8am-1pm

㉟ Basekamp

The Warehouse, Kings Lane, Swansea, SA1 2AQ
07833 208595
◉ basekampswansea

This particular base camp is a perfect place to pitch yourself for the day, laptop at the ready, with a plan to grind out some serious work while fuelled by top-notch speciality coffee and sweet sustenance.

The converted warehouse setting is so worth hunting out (it's not the easiest to find) for its airy Scandi-style interiors with cosy sofas, open-plan seating and abundant electrical sockets. It's also got a large outside area that's shady in summer, so it's no surprise Basekamp is popular with students, WFHers and those catching up with friends over a good brew.

🌟 Don't leave without bagging one of the T-shirts featuring collie Dylan driving the tuk-tuk

One of the quirkiest things about the experience is that the espresso (roasted in Bristol by Clifton Coffee) is pulled through a Conti Monte Carlo machine on a converted tuk-tuk. Weird, in a good way.

Beyond the banging flat whites, filter brews also feature – crafted in a rather more conventional style – and showcase coffee from the likes of Hard Lines, Campbell & Syme, Kiss the Hippo, Girls Who Grind and Extract. Many of the beans are also available to buy from the retail shelves.

Established
2020

Key roastery
Clifton Coffee Roasters

Brewing method
Espresso, V60, french press, cold brew, batch filter

Machine
Conti Monte Carlo

Grinder
Mahlkonig EK43

Opening hours
Mon-Fri
9am-3pm
Sat-Sun
9am-5pm
(seasonal opening hours)

(40) Storm in a Teacup Coffeehouse

Stall 59, Swansea Market, Union Street, Swansea, SA1 3PQ
07967 980778

storminateacupcoffeehouse

No trip to Swansea Market is complete without swinging by Storm in a Teacup to see what's brewing. In fact, as speciality is in short supply on this side of town, the small espresso and brew bar is the reason many coffee fans make the trip to Wales' largest indoor market.

Whether you're undertaking a planned pit stop or enjoying a chance encounter, a banging brew and a friendly chinwag with founder Ian Curtis awaits. Drawing on his 30 years of barista experience, Ian fashions beans from London's Square Mile into glossy espresso and batch brew. Recently, he's been experimenting by supercharging his line-up with Bloomin's mushroom blends – ask for a shot of the lion's mane or reishi in your coffee and see if you experience crystal-clear thinking (lion's mane) or a sense of tranquility (reishi).

⊙ Take your reusable cup (or *smug goblet*, as Ian calls it) for a sweet discount

If the weather's warm and a hot drink doesn't appeal, fruit-packed iced teas and affogatos make deliciously refreshing alternatives. Pair your pick of the drinks list with something sweet from a daily changing collection of local bakes that includes gooey brownies and syrupy flapjacks.

Established
2019

Key roastery
Square Mile Coffee Roasters

Brewing method
Espresso, filter

Machine
Victoria Arduino Black Eagle, Marco BRU F60M

Grinder
Victoria Arduino Mythos One, Mahlkonig EK43

Opening hours
Mon-Sat
8am-4pm

(41) Crafty Smuggler Coffee

82a Western Street, Sandfields, Swansea, SA1 3JS
craftysmugglercoffee.co.uk | 07402 018835
craftysmugglercoffee

There aren't many places in Swansea where you can savour a coffee that's been roasted in the city, so be sure to add Crafty Smuggler's clutch of roastery cafes to your Google Map faves.

This tiny coffee shop was the roastery's first outlet and is housed in a former garage on Western Street. Its younger brother (equally diminutive) can be found in student-central Uplands. You can also bag a Crafty flat white at the collab with Cwtch in out-of-town shopping centre McArthur Glen, near Bridgend.

The Crafty Smuggler baristas use beans from the roastery across town to create well-crafted brews. Play it safe (but smart) by opting for house espresso The Full Barrel, a smooth blend of beans from El Salvador, Ethiopia and Colombia. It yields notes of cocoa and nuts when paired with milk, and hints of orange when served black. If you're up for something different, ask about the latest single-origin release for a palate-expanding experience.

🌱 Pick up a bag of Crafty Smuggler beans for your home hopper

The coffee shop has a smattering of indoor and outdoor seating from which you can leisurely sip your pick of the coffee menu and tuck into one of the sweet or savoury bakes from the countertop selection. At the Uplands outlet, a bacon roll and a choice coffee are the only way to start the day.

Established
2023

Key roastery
Crafty Smuggler Coffee

Brewing method
Espresso

Machine
Conti Monte Carlo

Grinder
Eureka Zenith

Opening hours
Tue-Sat
8am-4pm
Sun
9am-3pm

42 Duck & Dough

37 Marlborough Road, Brynmill, Swansea, SA2 0DZ
07757 116730
duck.and.dough

The corner site that's home to Duck & Dough was boarded up for a quarter of a century until Max Freitas breathed new life into it and transformed it into a contemporary cafe.

In a short time, this unique coffee hangout (identifiable from outer space due to its giant flying-duck mural on the side of the building) has carved a niche for itself by serving top-notch speciality coffee that brings a taste of Brazil (Max's birthplace) to Brynmill.

Every Wednesday the team serve authentic Brazilian dishes such as pão de queijo (chewy tapioca cheese rolls), bolo de milho (sweet and buttery corn cake) and classic crème caramel.

☕ Off-piste pastel de nata variations include raspberry, chocolate and coconut

Unusual dishes and easy-going service, paired with Brazilian beats and beans, conjure up a laid-back vibe that's like spending time in the Tropics.

Natas by Max is the founder's other venture, which explains the unreal pastéis de nata stocking the bakes cabinet. The house-made golden-topped tarts feature crisp pastry, velvety custard and a touch of cinnamon, and make a wicked pairing for the syrupy espresso crafted from Bridge Coffee Roasters' beans.

Established
2024

Key roastery
Bridge Coffee Roasters

Brewing method
Espresso

Machine
Sanremo Zoe

Grinder
Anfim Milano

Opening hours
Mon-Fri
8.30am-4pm
Sat
9am-3pm
Sun
9am-1pm

(43) Sloth Coffee Co.

102 Glanmor Road, Uplands, Swansea, SA2 0QB
slothcoffeeco.com | 07759 506441
sloth.coffee.co

Rarely has a cafe name better explained the default vibe of an experience. Chilled to the point of being horizontal, Sloth has become one of Swansea's fave laidback hangouts, with owners (and brothers) Harry and Dai making a big impact on the community in which they grew up.

With backgrounds in carpentry, the duo built Sloth from the ground up, and set among the handbuilt wooden shelves and furniture are masses of happy houseplants that create a home-from-home atmos.

Wood skills aside, the brothers are hell bent on ensuring the coffee is what really nails their reputation. Guest espressos and filter coffees are changed weekly and rep a whole range of UK and international roasteries.

🕒 Strike up a caffeine convo with one of the baristas; they'll tip you the wink if anything special is brewing

Sloth works with quality local producers to source everything from milk to pastries, but its most notable collab is with vegan crumbsmiths Rhannu Bakery. While the counter is refreshed regularly with freshly baked vegan carbs, they're often snaffled within a couple of hours.

A small retail space gives customers the opportunity to take a slice of the experience home and includes beans, branded refillable coffee jars and graphic tees.

Established
2022

Key roastery
Clifton Coffee Roasters

Brewing method
Espresso, V60, batch brew, Orea, AeroPress, cold brew

Machine
Victoria Arduino Black Eagle Maverick

Grinder
Mahlkonig E65 GbW,
Mahlkonig E80 GbW,
Mahlkonig EK43

Opening hours
Mon-Fri
7am-2pm
Sat
8am-1pm
Sun
9am-1pm

Saint Hugo

㊹ **Saint Hugo**

Swing by Swansea's new cathedral to carbs for trad French pastries crafted by *Masterchef: The Professionals* contestant and leading pastry chef Ben Condé. Crisp croissants and their laminated mates are perfect paired with the house brew from Triple Co in Bristol. Find the original HQ in Llanelli.

11 St Mary's Square, SA1 3LP

saint-hugo.co.uk 📷 sainthugobakery ✂

㊻ **Square Peg Coffee House**

In need of a little soul nourishment? Visit this longstanding community cafe, which donates profits from its quality brews and tasty food to charity.

29b Gower Road, Sketty, Swansea, SA2 9BX

squarepeg.org.uk 📷 squarepegcoffee

㊺ **Ground Plant Based Coffee**

Paddlers still salty from the surf drop into this plant-based speciality coffee shop within The Sup Hut to revive with expertly prepped brews and homemade bakes.

The Sup Hut, Francis Street, Swansea, SA1 4NH

groundcoffeeswansea.com 📷 groundswansea

(47) Mumbles Coffee

34-36 Newton Road, Mumbles, Swansea, SA3 4AX

mumblescoffee.co.uk

mumblescoffee

Since moving up the road from its smaller spot in a nearby arcade, the Mumbles Coffee experience has gone from strength to strength.

This larger site is located in a roomy old telephone exchange building with views of Oystermouth Castle. It's been refurbed with style and is usually thrumming with activity as locals and tourists gather to scoff good grub and sink beautifully prepared speciality coffee.

The brews in question are crafted using a bespoke roast made specially for the crew by Lincoln & York. Drink it as espresso – the flat white is knockout – or sample the work of guest roasteries Extract, Poblado, Skylark and Ozone as batch brew or V60.

💡 Psst! A preorder click and collect service is launching soon

Sweet treats like the homemade granola and banana cake (both available to take away) are bolstered by a savoury menu of brunch and lunch classics like oozy cheese sourdough toasties and baked eggs. Produce is sourced locally wherever possible, so the sourdough comes from Little Valley in Swansea and bacon from Tuckers Butchers down the road.

If all the tables are full, hit the grab-and-go area for a takeaway and feast on your spoils down on the seafront.

Established
2013

Key roastery
Lincoln & York

Brewing method
Espresso, V60, batch brew

Machine
Synesso Hydra, Victoria Arduino Eagle One

Grinder
Mahlkonig E65S GbW x 4, Mahlkonig E80 GbW, Mahlkonig Guatemala

Opening hours
Mon-Sat
7am-4pm
Sun
9am-2pm

Microlot by Mumbles Coffee

28 Dunns Lane, Mumbles, Swansea, SA3 4AA
mumblescoffee.co.uk
microlot_

This cosy little satellite of Mumbles Coffee's larger cafe on Newton Road is where those in the know head for a speedy caffeine hit when the queue's out the door at the big-sister site.

Set back from the seafront between pastel-coloured fishing cottages, Microlot is the perfect place to escape the crowds and savour a cup of house-roasted coffee.

The house blend is a well-balanced curation of Central American and Indian coffees which delivers a rounded body with subtle caramel sweetness, earthy chocolate notes and a clean finish. It's joined by guest beans from roasteries such as Ozone, Extract and Poblado which are served as espresso or V60 pourover. Beans are also available to buy – ask the baristas to grind them to your desired spec.

● Try the buttery kouign-amann with a smooth flat white

These brews are best paired with one of the freshly made pastries that crowd the counter. Special attention should be paid to the pastéis de nata made by Max of Duck and Dough. On Saturdays, Gower Doughnut's bakes arrive by the trayload.

When the weather's good, the glass panels are removed from the windows, allowing the sea breeze to mingle with the fresh coffee aromas. Or pull up a pew outside for full-on sun worshipping with a fresh-fruit smoothie.

Established
2021

Key roastery
Lincoln & York

Brewing method
Espresso, V60

Machine
Modbar Espresso AV

Grinder
Mahlkonig E65S GbW x 2, Mahlkonig EK43

Opening hours
Mon-Sat
8am-3pm
Sun
8am-1pm

49) **Fikamumbles**

Love Round Hill coffee? Sucker for a good cocktail? Big fan of bagels? If it's a yes to any one – or all – of the above, stop what you're doing and head to this new day-to-night cafe.

44 Newton Road, Swansea, SA3 6BQ

fikamumbles

50) **Boo's Kitchen**

(Mostly) veggie and vegan dishes crafted with fresh ingredients and homemade elements always hit the spot at Boo's. Cheerful bonhomie and speciality pours bump the experience up a notch, too.

2 Woodville Road, The Mumbles, Swansea, SA3 4AD

boosmumbles

51) **Motley Pie**

Looking for a decent cup of Clifton Coffee with a slab of cake, homemade cookie or savoury pie on the side? This takeaway-only Gowerton pie shop will be your jam. Try the homemade house spesh breakfast pie: a pastry shell crammed with bacon, sausage and beans, topped with a hash brown lid.

Woodlands, Gowerton, Swansea, SA4 3DP

motleypie.co.uk motley.pie

52 Outside The Box

Unit 4-5, 4 Prydwen Road, Fforestfach, Swansea, SA5 4HN
 otb.coffee

This spanking new opening in Fforestfach can be tracked down on an industrial estate at the 179 CrossFit gym. *Train inside the box, fuel Outside The Box* is their unofficial slogan and visitors can grab a spot that's literally outside the black shipping container box and sip brews as they enjoy top tunes.

OTB's post-workout coffee-club members make up the lion's share of the clientele but everyone, including four-legged friends, is welcome. On sunny days, don't be surprised to find Lycra-clad coffee drinkers celebrating their latest PBs with quality sips while they watch those still in pumping-iron mode in the outdoor gym.

◉ Don't miss the fresh homemade sandos and subs crammed with special fillings

Caffeinated rewards come courtesy of Welsh roasters Hard Lines, which creates the speciality blends, while temptation on the counter includes croissants, traybakes and pies. You've probably earnt it, right?

Established
2025

Key roastery
Hard Lines

Brewing method
Espresso, batch brew

Machine
Rocket Boxer

Grinder
Anfim Luna

Opening hours
Mon-Fri
7am-2pm
Sat
8.30am-12pm
Sun
9am-1.30pm

(53) Lle Tarw

Brecon Road, Ynyswen, Swansea, SA9 1YR
07837 137705
lletarw_2023

Road-tripping to picturesque Bannau Brycheiniog? You'll want to pull into this motor-themed coffee shop for a speciality refuel en route.

Throughout the space, carefully considered interior decor and furnishings celebrate motor culture – from the array of global number plates and retro artwork on the walls to the spanner teaspoons. The result is a rustic-yet-cosy environment in which to chinwag with other motorists while guzzling the good stuff.

Coaltown Coffee Roasters' Black Gold is the house blend that keeps the Mahlkonig grinders busy, before Lle Tarw's baristas fashion it into a range of silky brews via a sleek La Marzocco.

⚡ Supercharge your adventures with a brew and locally made cake or sausage roll

Coaltown also supplies a second coffee which rotates with the seasons, and guest roastery Ride & Grind in Edinburgh occasionally features with its aptly named Motor Oil or Rocket Fuel blends.

Don't be surprised to find classic or performance cars parked up outside – Lle Tarw often hosts events for petrolheads and is also a natural meeting point for bikers exploring nearby beauty spots.

Established
2023

Key roastery
Coaltown Coffee Roasters

Brewing method
Espresso, filter

Machine
La Marzocco Linea PB

Grinder
Mahlkonig E65S GbW, Mahlkonig EK43 S

Opening hours
Mon-Sun
8.30am–6pm
(seasonal opening hours)

SOUTH ROAST-ERIES

Hard Lines | **p79**

54 Rate of Rise Coffee

15a Nevill Street, Abergavenny, Monmouthshire, NP7 5AA

rateofrisecoffee.co.uk

rateofrisecoffeeroaster

Perched on the edge of Bannau Brycheiniog, Rate of Rise is the only coffee roastery in Monmouthshire and is hidden away inside a walled garden in the middle of Abergavenny. In summer, it's surrounded by colourful blooms while, in winter, it rocks cosy cabin vibes.

Established
2024

Roaster make & size
Dalian Amazon 1kg

'A boozy natural Ugandan coffee which delivers a taste of the Tropics'

The mission is to roast exemplary beans from farmers around the world with the highest environmental standards, so the coffee is either sourced directly or through small importers with meaningful and transparent trade relationships with growers. The results can be experienced in a beautiful Brazilian house roast with notes of chocolate, hazelnut and butterscotch, or a boozy natural Ugandan which delivers a taste of the Tropics.

In line with the team's green creds, all the packaging is compostable. Rate of Rise also supports local tree-planting charity Stump Up For Trees, with the aim of ensuring this leafy region of Wales remains verdant.

Visitors can visit to see the magic happen at the roastery cafe, where they'll also meet new team member Fern the puppy.

55 Hard Lines

Unit 8 Gwaelod y Garth, Cardiff, CF15 8LA

hard-lines.co.uk

hardlinescoffee

Coffee, people and creativity are the guiding principles of this South Wales roasting powerhouse. From responsible sourcing to sustainable roasting, Hard Lines founders Sophie Smith and Matt Jones put community first, whether that's close to home or at origin, and like to do things a little differently.

Since its launch in 2017, the roastery has rocketed to the upper echelons of speciality society, and its coffee can be found in the hoppers of some of the best cafes in the UK and beyond. While Hard Lines has received great praise (including being shortlisted for a Sprudge Design Award and plenty of mentions in the press), the team haven't let success go to their heads and continue to roast accessible coffee that everyone can enjoy.

'The roastery has rocketed to the upper echelons of speciality society'

'We like to showcase the coffees we love to drink, share our knowledge and are always ready to learn,' says Sophie.

For a seriously good selection of eats, quirky merch and the full range of coffee serves, head to the Hard Lines cafe in Canton, which slings shots, pours juicy batch brew and carbs up Cardiffians all week long. Looking to upskill in coffee? Check out Hard Lines' website for upcoming home barista courses and roastery tours.

Established
2017

Roaster make & size
Loring S15
Falcon 15kg,
Loring S35
Kestrel 35kg

56 Welsh Coffee Co.

Unit 4 Kingswood Court, Ogmore Road,
Ogmore-by-Sea, Vale of Glamorgan, CF35 5BP

welshcoffee.com | welshcoffeeco

It's no coincidence this eco-minded roastery is just a stone's skim from the beach. Founder Huw Williams moved Welsh Coffee Co. to the coastal town of Ogmore-by-Sea to be closer to his local community – and to check the surf from his desk.

Sustainability is paramount for Huw, who established Welsh Coffee Co. in 2011 to reflect his passion for the great outdoors and pursuits such as surfing, walking and yoga. The roastery runs on solar power and flame-roasts beans in Probat roasters.

'Aur/Gold is another winning blend, revealing a symphony of chocolate, caramel and apricot notes'

The line-up includes multiple Great Taste award winners, among them two-star coffees Mor and Bendigedig – South American blends with chocolate notes and a touch of tropical fruit. Aur/Gold is another winning blend, revealing a symphony of chocolate, caramel and apricot notes. The single-origin selection zones in on the Americas and features beans from Nicaragua and Colombia.

Sample the brews at Welsh Coffee Co.'s cafe in Ogmore's community hall, or book an appointment at the roastery cafe to see the bronzing in action.

Established
2011

Roaster make & size
Probat 25kg,
Probat 15kg

57 Kontext Coffee Company

This roastery near Monmouth keeps locals both sides of the border well caffeinated via sustainably sourced beans. Visit the roastery for brews, cookies and freshly roasted coffee on Tuesday and Thursday mornings.

Wyastone Business Park, Wyastone Leys, Ganarew, NP25 3SR

kontextcoffee.com kontextcoffeecompany

58 Scout Coffee Roasters

Good deeds is the Scout Coffee Roasters motto and the Newport crew live up to the ethos by donating some profits to charity, planting a tree for each order and providing carbon-neutral shipping – and that's before you factor in the joyful range of beans it creates.

8 Evtol Trading Estate, Frederick St, Newport, NP20 2DR

scoutcoffee.co.uk scout_coffee_roasters

59 Double Trouble Coffee Roasters

Kickstarted by sisters Gail and Emma, micro roastery Double Trouble is the result of their shared love of speciality coffee. Their range of direct-trade beans include releases from unsung coffee-growing countries like Indonesia and Vietnam.

25 Heol Las, North Cornelly, Bridgend, CF33 4AP

doubletroublecoffee.co.uk
 double_trouble_coffee

Green Bridge of Wales / Pont Werdd Cymru

MID & WEST

Mid & West Wales

● Coffee shops

60	Greenhouse Cafe & Kitchen
61	Narrative Coffee
62	Georgie Porgies
63	Latte-Da
64	Shire Coffee at HWYL
65	Shire Coffee at The Bookshop
66	T-Boi Coffee
67	Humble Coffi
68	Coaltown Espresso Bar
69	Pitchfork & Provision
70	Bay Coffee Roasters Cafe
71	Diod
72	HMY
73	Get the Boys a Lift
74	The Gourmet Pig
75	Nook & Noble
76	Crwst
77	Coffi a Bara
78	Gwesty Cymru
79	Baravin
80	Caffi Castell Harlech
81	Two Islands
82	Caffi Siop Plas

● Roasteries

83	Cribyn Coffee Company
84	Coaltown Coffee Roasters
85	Bay Coffee Roasters
86	Dyfi Roastery
87	Blue Monday Coffee
88	Ffa Da Coffee

Locations are approximate

Greenhouse Cafe & Kitchen

King's Nurseries, Garthmyl, Montgomery, Powys, SY15 6RT
greenhousecafeandkitchen.co.uk | 01686 641939
greenhousecafeandkitchen

© Brad Carr Photography

This garden-centre cafe is the kind of oasis of greenery and beanery that green-fingered coffee lovers dream of.

Situated in a verdant countryside spot next to King's Nurseries, every detail has been meticulously designed to deliver a lush sensory experience.

When the team first dreamt up the concept of the purpose-built space, they opted for floor-to-ceiling windows so visitors could soak up the picturesque scenery while sitting in contemporary interiors and indulging in produce-led dishes and speciality coffee. Their vision paid off and quickly captured the attention of others – and saw them scoop the 2024 Powys Business Start-Up Award.

💡 Don't leave without picking up a loaf of springy Greenhouse sourdough to-go

The house beans are a Hundred House Coffee blend, which detonates a chocolate bomb in every espresso while pairing perfectly with steamed Daisy Bank Dairy milk. A rotating selection of speciality blends, plus a cracking decaf from Hundred House, are also available.

While the coffee is top-drawer, it's actually the food that has caused Greenhouse's popularity to bloom. A tempting menu is split into signature, brunch, small plates and sides. Will it be the braised spiced lamb flatbread or turkish eggs with chilli oil and sourdough that accompany your flat white? Decisions, decisions ...

Established
2022

Key roastery
Hundred House Coffee

Brewing method
Espresso

Machine
La Marzocco Linea S

Grinder
Mahlkonig E65S GbW, PUQ Press M3

Opening hours
Mon-Sun
9am-4pm
(kitchen open 9am-2pm)

(61) Narrative Coffee

Glan Wye House, West Street, Rhayader, Powys, LD6 5AD

narrativecoffee.co.uk

narrativecoffeeuk

The stimulating array of brews at this next-gen coffee house in Rhayader entices speciality coffee fans from far and wide.

Owner Sam Lunn's experience working in the speciality industry has equipped him with the skills and confidence to create a fresh kind of coffee shop. The London Coffee Masters 2025 finalist doesn't affiliate with any one roastery, instead rotating single guest roasters to keep the flavour wheel spinning and support as many indie roasteries as possible (beans are also available to buy). The partnerships often result in collaborative coffees bespoke to Narrative.

There are usually five roasts and six brew methods to choose from, and the expertly trained baristas are brilliant at matching customers with beans and styles to suit their palate.

ⓘ Can't find anywhere to perch? A secret staircase leads to more basement seating

No one should feel intimidated, however, as there isn't a hint of snobbery in this Narrative. Sam and his gang go by the rule: *customer first, coffee second*, so visitors' pleasure is paramount – even when the baristas are asked for a brew served blazing hot or super sweet. With its cosy living-room vibe, it's no wonder this place is popular or that there are plans in place for a sister site.

Visitors should make excellent use of their caffeine high by taking a post-coffee hike up nearby Elan Valley.

Established
2024

Key roastery
Multiple roasteries

Brewing method
Espresso, filter, V60, Chemex, Clever Dripper, cafetiere

Machine
La Marzocco Linea Classic S

Grinder
Mahlkonig EK Omnia, Anfim Pratica, Fiorenzato F83 E Pro x 2

Opening hours
Mon-Sun
8am-5pm

© Radu Dumitrescu

62 Georgie Porgies

It's not just the toothsome cakes that keep customers coming back to Georgie's. The caffeination is on-point and the surroundings cute and cosy.

21 High Street, Builth Wells, Powys, LD2 3DL

georgieporgiescoffee

63 Latte-Da

As its name suggests, the luscious lattes crafted from Extract beans here demand attention. Sip a brew in the secluded botanical garden out back then venture forth into the Bannau Brycheiniog.

Beaufort Street, Crickhowell, Powys, NP8 1AD

latte-da-crickhowell.co.uk

latte.da.crickhowell

(64) Shire Coffee at HWYL

20 Market Street, Llanelli, Carmarthenshire, SA15 1YD
shire.coffee | 01554 775537
hwyl.shire

The coffee experience at what was formerly just Hwyl has gone great guns since the Shire Coffee team took over in 2023 and slid in their elevated speciality offering alongside Hwyl's much-loved brunch line-up.

The cafe is busier than ever with punters pairing the house-fave flat white with dishes such as cockles, bacon and laverbread served with eggs, black pudding and toasted sourdough. Another popular pastime involves matching a batch brew or V60 with a full-Welsh Brecwast or its little brother, Brecwast Bach.

🧭 Feast on a globetrotting array of cuisines at the regular pop-up evenings

The coffee accompanying these edibles is roasted by Triple Co Roast, although Round Hill, Yallah, Cairngorm and Dark Arts also star. The barista team are big fans of juicy Kenyan coffees and owner Seb Osborne says: *'If there's a roaster with Kenyan beans on their list, the chances are you'll find it in our guest-roast hopper.'*

The big news is that the team recently opened another site, Shire Coffee at The Bookshop, just across town. Swing by to crack the spine of a new book and revel in more caffeine and cake thrills.

Established
2023

Key roastery
Triple Co Roast

Brewing method
Espresso,
batch brew, V60

Machine
La Marzocco Linea PB

Grinder
Mahlkonig E65S GbW,
Mahlkonig E65S

Opening hours
Mon-Sat
9am-3pm

65 Shire Coffee at The Bookshop

57-59 Stepney Street, Llanelli, Carmarthenshire, SA15 3YA
shire.coffee

shire.coffee

Shire Coffee just started a new chapter with the opening of a second bricks-and-mortar site in Llanelli.

Such has been the success of Shire Coffee at Hwyl that the team felt confident in opening this beautiful little coffee shop across town. You won't find it serving the mega brunch dishes of its big sister, but The Bookshop is a delightful place to appreciate the Shire Coffee team's on-point bean and brew expertise while munching a cake or bake.

🏴󠁧󠁢󠁷󠁬󠁳󠁿 Visit the sister site at Hwyl for a delicious breakfast and more adventures in coffee

The team have entirely transformed the space and given it an elegant bookshop-inspired makeover that includes plenty of — you guessed it — books.

The interiors were designed by owner Seb's sister and include two specially crafted booths where laptop warriors can grind out their next magnum opus … or simply catch up on emails.

Visit for carefully crafted espresso, batch and filter coffees from roasteries including Triple Co Roast, Round Hill, Yallah, Dark Arts and Red Bank.

Established
2025

Key roastery
Triple Co Roast

Brewing method
Espresso, batch filter

Machine
La Marzocco Linea PB

Grinder
Mahlkonig E65S GbW

Opening hours
Tue-Fri
8am-2pm
Sat-Sun
(check social media for more information)

# 66 T-Boi Coffee

Primavera Wellness Space, 3 West End, Llanelli, Carmarthenshire, SA15 3DN

 primavera_wellness_space

T-Boi Coffee is a proudly trans-owned, fully inclusive wellness space and coffee hub for the LGBTQIA+ community – and everyone else besides.

In collaboration with the local council, it's also a Warm Hub and provides a welcoming and inclusive spot where refreshments are free on Thursdays.

Beyond all this community-focused spirit, T-Boi's trans-man barista Jay-Harley Rees also serves up cracking brews and is known and loved in this patch of Wales for upping the quality of caffeination on offer.

ⓘ Stressed out? Book an on-site massage or holistic therapy

T-Boi prides itself on devising unique takes on traditional coffees serves. For an exotic twist on a milky favourite, try the vegan Spanish latte: an uber-creamy concoction made with condensed coconut milk, two shots of espresso and silkily textured coconut milk.

Plant-based sweet treats are sourced from local small bakeries, with the likes of vegan cruffins and pain suisse providing fuel for the army of WFH-ers who've made the cafe their home-from-home for its quality caffeine and carbs.

Established
2022

Key roastery
The Whitford Coffee Co.

Brewing method
Espresso, cafetiere, pourover, drip

Machine
SAB Jolly

Grinder
Fracino

Opening hours
Thu
10am-2pm
Fri
3pm-7pm
Sat
11am-4pm
(seasonal opening hours)

67 Humble Coffi

Unit 2 Stradey District Centre, Maes Y Coed, Llanelli, Carmarthenshire, SA15 4EB
humblecoffi.co.uk
humblecoffi

BEEN THERE · BEEN THERE · BEEN THERE · BEEN THERE ·

Coffee fans, yoga mums, retirees and Gen Zers all flock to this insider's find a stone's throw from the former Stradey Park stadium. Make tracks to the unassuming coffee house to join them in the industrial-style space for cracking coffee and food.

The Humble experience is high quality, but it isn't pretentious. This is a laidback, friendly spot where customers can sip a velvety Clifton espresso and appreciate the flavours of a well-prepared AeroPress made with guest beans ground in a Helios grinder. Off-piste coffee creations include the rosemary and sea-salt mocha.

⚡ Swing by on a Saturday night for cocktails and tapas

If you're dithering over which dish to pick from the all-day menu, the Chicken Clwb — Humble's chicken, bacon and halloumi twist on the classic club sarnie — is happiness on a plate. Looking for something lighter? Try the smoked salmon sourdough slathered in cream cheese and sprinkled with pink pickled onions and dukkah.

Whatever you choose, it would be remiss not to leave a little space for one of the tempting pastries, cakes or plant-based bakes on the counter. Resistance is futile when faced with the fan-favourite cinnamon swirl.

Established
2019

Key roastery
Clifton Coffee Roasters

Brewing method
Espresso, filter, AeroPress

Machine
Sanremo Verona

Grinder
Mahlkonig E65S Gbw, Eureka Helios 65

Opening hours
Mon, Thu-Fri
7.30am-4pm
Sat
7.30am-10.30pm
Sun
10am-4pm

Llanelli

Coaltown Espresso Bar

The Roastery, Foundry Road, Ammanford, Carmarthenshire, SA18 2LS
coaltowncoffee.co.uk | 01269 400105
coaltowncoffee

Coffee fans exploring Wales might expect to find a single speciality coffee shop in a town this far west, but to encounter a speciality roastery with training academy and espresso bar is somewhat eyebrow raising.

Not that so many people just stumble upon Coaltown anymore. The roastery has become such a well-loved player on the Welsh coffee scene that brew geeks now make a pilgrimage to visit its open-plan HQ on the outskirts of Ammanford. As well as hosting the roastery (which supplies cafes, restaurants and indie businesses across Wales), it's also the home of Coaltown's espresso bar and a training space where locals and visitors gather to sample the latest house blends and single origins and learn how to prepare them at home.

● Coffee drinkers can now have their Coaltown beans delivered to their local InPost locker

Black Gold is the house espresso blend and where the Coaltown story began in 2014. The current version is the third iteration and a great place for first-timers to start.

Founder Scott James has always been passionate about his local community and created the Ammanford hub in his hometown so he could employ people from this rural area. In 2019 he secured B Corp status for the business.

Established
2014

Key roastery
Coaltown
Coffee Roasters

Brewing method
Espresso

Machine
La Marzocco KB90

Grinder
Mahlkonig EK43,
Mahlkonig E65S × 2

Opening hours
Mon-Sun
8am-4pm

69 Pitchfork & Provision

Castle Courtyard, 113 Rhosmaen Street, Llandeilo, Carmarthenshire, SA19 6HN
pitchforkandprovision.wales | 07886 447276
pitchfork.and.provision

Speciality coffee and sourdough are the headline acts at this cafe, bakery and patisserie in picturesque Llandeilo, where Welsh-speaking staff can give you the lowdown on brewspeak, Cymru-style.

Each perfectly risen loaf is made from scratch by the Pitchfork & Provision bakers over the course of 36 hours. Their special recipe uses a ten-year-old levain starter and a blend of Shipton Mill white, wholemeal and rye flours, plus a little sea salt and water. Once ready, the artisan homebaked breads are used as the base for multiple scrumptious lunch dishes.

❂ Load up on cheese and charcuterie to-go from the hidden-gem deli counter

The house espresso, a single-origin washed coffee from Sidamo in Ethiopia, is lightly roasted by the pros at Coaltown Coffee Roasters. It was specifically handpicked by the P&P team to complement the distinctive flavours of the house sourdough, as well as the ever-changing array of pastries and sweet bakes that line the counter of one of the few artisan bakeries that specialises in viennoiserie in Carmarthenshire.

Established
2020

Key roastery
Coaltown Coffee Roastery

Brewing method
Espresso, batch filter

Machine
La Marzocco GB5 S

Grinder
Mahlkonig E65S GbW

Opening hours
Mon (bank holidays only)
9am-3pm
Tue-Sat
9am-4pm
Sun
9am-3pm

70 Bay Coffee Roasters Cafe

Unit 4, 41-45 Richmond Terrace, Carmarthen, SA31 1HG

baycoffeeroasters.com

baycoffeeroasters

Having supplied cafes with award-winning beans for years, in 2024 the Bay Coffee Roasters' team decided to open their own spot where they could serve coffee their way. They took on this Carmarthen cafe from one of their customers, keeping the dedicated team in place while giving the space a glow-up.

Being in control of the coffee's journey, from sourcing to roasting and serving, equals meticulous attention to detail and does justice to the farmers at origin.

These quality brews, when combined with friendly, knowledgeable staff and a wide selection of speciality beans for sale, means caffeine seekers are ensured of a top-notch experience.

Check out the cafe's Rubasse Nano roaster – the team use it to experiment with small-batch profiles

Not sure where to dive in? Greet the day with a luscious brew made using Bay's single-origin Time Machine coffee. The Great Taste award-winning coffee hails from Brazil, where the beans are pulped and dried – a natural process that provides its distinctively creamy body, nutty bite and lingering sweet finish.

Established
2024

Key roastery
Bay Coffee Roasters

Brewing method
Espresso

Machine
Slayer Steam EP

Grinder
Eureka Helios 65

Opening hours
Mon-Sun
8am-4pm

(71) **Diod**

This Welsh coffee shop with Scandi-style interiors is a great place for soaking up the Cymraeg vibe (90 per cent of the team speak Welsh) and gulping delish Gower-roasted coffee.

135 Rhosmaen Street, Llandeilo,
Carmarthenshire, SA19 6EN

diod.cymru diodllandeilo

(72) **HMY**

Sip on-point espressos and check out kaleidoscopic custom boots, shoes and jerseys at this part coffee house, part custom artwork and clothing brand.

41-45 Richmond Terrace, Carmarthen,
Carmarthenshire, SA31 1HG

hmycustoms.co.uk  hmy_customs

Get the Boys a Lift

40 Bridge Street, Haverfordwest, Pembrokeshire, SA61 2AD
gtbal.co.uk
gettheboysalift

Ever felt guilty about the amount you spend on coffee? Clear your conscience with a trip to this groundbreaking cafe in Haverfordwest, where you can simultaneously sip and support a fantastic cause.

The community hub provides a safe space and – remarkably – free counselling and mental health support to people in the area, which is partly funded by the brews and merch sold in the GTBAL coffee shop.

The team sling 'spros from a La Marzocco Linea machine, transforming the bespoke house blend, crafted by the roasters at Allpress, into velvety flat whites, cappuccinos and lattes. Pop in to pick up a takeaway coffee and browse a retail offering that includes bags of the house coffee, branded tees, hoodies and hats.

The stylish cafe space (check out the beautiful – and own-built – polished concrete bar) also features a What's On board of free services, such as drug and alcohol support, CV-writing classes and work experience. Upstairs, therapy rooms deliver the work funded by the banging brews.

◉ Want to support GTBAL but can't make it to Pembrokeshire? Make a donation online

The GTBAL experience also hits the road via a mobile coffee van that parks up at Freshwater West between April and October and appears at festivals and events throughout the year. A La Marzocco Linea Mini and Mythos One grinder have the mobile baristas set to serve top-notch coffee in any terrain.

Established
2019

Key roastery
Allpress Espresso

Brewing method
Espresso

Machine
La Marzocco
Linea Classic

Grinder
Victoria Arduino
Mythos One

Opening hours
Mon-Fri
7.30am-4.30pm
Sat
9am-3pm

(74) The Gourmet Pig

32 West Street, Fishguard, Pembrokeshire, SA65 9AD
gourmetpig.co.uk | 01348 874404
gourmetpigcoffeeco

Visitors to Fishguard on the hunt for decent coffee are usually directed by locals straight to The Gourmet Pig, a speciality deli and coffee shop in the heart of the town.

Once the smell of freshly ground coffee has lured them through the door, the magnetic pull of piles of delicious artisan produce entices them to linger. An assortment of chutneys, jams, olive oils, vinegars and wines line the shelves, while fresh breads, cheeses, salads, quiches and antipasti adorn the counter.

☕ Grab a bag of Gourmet Pig coffee beans to continue the caffeine thrills at home

The indoor seating area is small, but those who find a seat can pick a record from the vinyl collection and get a spin on the turntable. Once you've selected your soundtrack, pair it with a doorstep of ciabatta stuffed with Preseli Mountain-reared Dexter brisket, gruyère, cornichons and Toloja Orchards mustard, plus a cup of the deli's own Peru-Honduras blend.

The Gourmet Pig follows a low-food-miles philosophy, so lots of the ingredients are sourced locally. The team has also introduced a zero-waste area where customers can stock up on refills of muesli, beans, pulses, nuts and coffee beans.

Established
2009

Key roastery
The Gourmet Pig Coffee Co

Brewing method
Espresso, drip

Machine
Conti Monte Carlo

Grinder
Mahlkonig, Mazzer Super Jolly × 2

Opening hours
Mon-Fri
9.30am-4.30pm
Sat
9.30am-4pm

⑦⑤ Nook & Noble

Unit 15, Canolfan Teifi, Pendre, Cardigan, Ceredigion, SA43 1JL
nookandnoble.com
◉ nookandnoblecafe

This new addition to the coffeeverse has further upped the speciality serves on offer in Ceredigion and the historic town of Cardigan.

Owner and barista Rob Ross was bitten by the speciality coffee bug in Australia 15 years ago and became so enamoured that he retrained as a barista and roaster, role-hopping in the industry until he launched Nook & Noble.

Demand has been so strong since opening that Rob and his team have taken over an empty arcade space next door to enable them to introduce a new lounge, kids' play area and games room.

☕ Keep 'em peeled on socials for in-house coffee cuppings

As a multi-roaster cafe, N&N likes to spread the love and always has beans from different roasteries in the hoppers. Faves include The Barn, La Cabra, Colonna, Prodigal and Tim Wendelboe. The choice doesn't end there: the cafe offers a frozen-bean menu of over 100 coffees and seven brew methods.

Peckish? The legendary almond croissants have a local reputation all of their own. For something more substantial, check out the gourmet toppings on toast, healthy salad bar and sausage rolls served with a side of crunchy slaw.

Established
2024

Key roastery
Multiple roasteries

Brewing method
Espresso, pourover, Kalita Wave, Orea, Clever Dripper, batch brew, Paragon

Machine
La Marzocco Linea Mini

Grinder
Mahlkonig E65S GbW, Mahlkonig EK43

Opening hours
Mon-Sat
9.30am-4pm
Sun
(check social media)

Crwst

 **Crwst**

Hotfoot it to this airy bakery-cafe to scoff sourdough, bakes and doughnuts while sipping Carmarthen's Bay coffee. Brunch starts at 10am but desperate early birds can bag a cinny bun and flattie first thing.

Priory Street, Cardigan, SA43 1BU

crwst.cymru 🅞 crwst.cymru

##

We'd never gatekeep a speciality coffee house with a bakery wing – especially one kneading goods as great as this Tregaron find.

Unit 4, Clos Twm, Sion Cati, Tregaron, Ceredigion, SY25 6JL

🅞 coffiabara

78 Gwesty Cymru

19 Marine Terrace, Aberystwyth, Ceredigion, SY23 2AZ
cymru.wales | 01970 564005
gwesty.cymru.aber

On the ground floor of recently reopened boutique hotel Gwesty Cymru is a rather excellent bar. With epic sea views over Cardigan Bay, it's a knockout setting for a glass of wine, craft beer, cocktail ... or expertly crafted coffee.

The all-day spot (it's open from 10am until late, seven days a week) is run by the young team behind Baravin restaurant and bar next door, and they pour the same level of care into their craft here as at the sister site.

☕ Head over in happy hour (4–7pm) to enjoy a glass of wine and a small plate for a tenner

On the coffee front, the crew are loyal to Welsh coffee miners Coaltown. Mosey over for a morning macchiato or lunchtime latte and you'll most likely be treated to the roastery's flagship Black Gold blend. It's a winning all-rounder with notes of biscuit and chocolate, plus the richness that comes from being hand-roasted to just beyond first crack.

Sunny day? Bag a perch outdoors on the sea-view terrace for the best seat in the house. Ease into evening by switching up your order to a Blackgold Espresso Martini (Coaltown espresso, Cariel Vanilla vodka, Kahlúa and panela sugar) or coffee-infused Negroni (Coaltown coffee, Campari, Tanqueray No. Ten and vermouth).

Established
2024

Key roastery
Coaltown Coffee Roaster

Brewing method
Espresso

Machine
La Marzocco Linea Mini

Grinder
Mahlkonig E65S

Opening hours
Mon-Sun
10am-late

79 Baravin

1 Llys Y Brenin, 1 Terrace Road, Aberystwyth, Ceredigion, SY23 2AP
baravin.co.uk | 01970 611189
baravinaber

It can be a tough call to find a restaurant that bookends a great meal with equally great caffeine, but Baravin got the memo. This venue on the Aber Prom serves quality seafood, pizzas, burgers, craft beer, cocktails and wine with a side order of exceptional speciality coffee.

The brews come courtesy of Coaltown in Ammanford, and the team have plumped for Black Gold, the roastery's flagship blend. The seasonal espresso is a perennial crowdpleaser for its nutty milk choc and biscuit notes. It's handroasted to just beyond first crack to give it a rich espresso zing while still retaining its natural flavours. Sit in and savour, or grab and go and take a stroll along the seafront while you slurp.

ⓘ Enjoy outstanding views of Cardigan Bay from the restaurant

There's every excuse to visit Baravin, regardless of the time of day. Head over first thing for an invigorating flat white and BV breakfast. Rock up at lunch for a cortado and a slice of pastrami, sauerkraut, mustard mayo and mozzarella pizza. Or ease into the evening by segueing from macchiato to Espresso Martini while picking at a charcuterie platter with pals.

That's not to say you can't visit purely for caffeination, but it would be criminal not to at least pair your brew with something from the cakes and bakes selection.

Established
2012

Key roastery
Coaltown Coffee Roasters

Brewing method
Espresso

Machine
La Marzocco Linea Classic

Grinder
Mahlkonig E65S

Opening hours
Mon-Sat
10am-late

⑳ Caffi Castell Harlech

Camera app at the ready: the speciality coffee serves in Edward I's fortress are served with a mighty backdrop of Eyri National Park — and gluttonous cakes. Soak it up and gulp it down.

Castle Square, Harlech, Gwynedd, LL46 2YH
cafficastell.co.uk 📷 cafficastellharlech

㉛ Two Islands

Feed caffeine and sugar cravings at this sleek ice cream parlour and coffee shop. Lap up a home-churned salted-coffee ice cream made with Coaltown espresso and flaky sea salt to fill two needs with one indulgent deed.

Bank Place, Lon Pen Cei, Abersoch, Gwynedd, LL53 7DW

twoislandsicecream.co.uk 📷 two__islands

㉜ Caffi Siop Plas

Scout out this cherry-red barn for pukka food and banging brews. The produce-led menu and tasty coffee is best enjoyed inside the former zinc shed, which is invitingly rustic.

Plas Carmel, Anelog, Pwllheli, Gwynedd, LL53 8LL
📷 caffisiopplas

WEST & MID ROAST-ERIES

Coaltown Coffee Roasters | p107

83 Cribyn Coffee Company

Scethrog House, Scethrog, Brecon, Powys, LD3 7EQ
cribyncoffeecompany.com | 07775 648152
cribyncoffee

From their beautifully restored 300-year-old coach house just outside Brecon, Rhys and Gwen Iley feed their obsession with speciality coffee by spending their days sourcing, bronzing and slurping.

The like-minded pair launched the roastery in 2021 and, to reflect their deep-rooted connection to the landscape they call home, they named it Cribyn after the iconic peak in Bannau Brycheiniog.

With decades of industry experience between them, Rhys and Gwen tap into their knowledge and contacts across the coffee-growing belt to source standout greens. The precious lots are then given a blast in the Probat for consistently expressive results.

'A roast profile that coaxes out rich notes of caramel and sweet cocoa, with the citrus twist of mandarin for lift'

Cribyn's signature release, Coach House No.1, is a single origin from Mió in Brazil: a family-run farm known for its sustainability creds and high-quality beans. Rhys and Gwen have honed a roast profile that coaxes out rich notes of caramel and sweet cocoa, with the citrus twist of mandarin for lift.

Cribyn's beans are available for both wholesale and domestic customers, providing a taste of the wild Welsh landscape for cafes and home kitchens.

Established
2020

Roaster make & size
Probat P12 12kg

© Daniel Alford

Brecon

84 Coaltown Coffee Roasters

The Roastery, Foundry Road, Ammanford, Carmarthenshire, SA18 2LS
coaltowncoffee.co.uk | 01269 400105
coaltowncoffee

The first speciality coffee roastery in the UK to earn B Corp status wasn't in London, Manchester or even Cardiff, but the former mining town of Ammanford in Carmarthenshire.

When Scott James established Coaltown Coffee in 2014, the founding principle was putting people and purpose above profit. So, once the coffee brand had built momentum and a burgeoning fanbase, Scott's next move was to establish an open-plan roastery, espresso bar and training academy in his home town of Ammanford. The aim was to create jobs for locals struggling to find work in such a rural location, and it's been a great success.

The industrial-style HQ is where Coaltown's broad spectrum of blends and single origins are roasted. The longstanding and seasonally changing house blend, Black Gold, is currently an intoxicating mix of beans from Brazil, Peru and Honduras. Those after something more unusual will enjoy exploring the roastery's shifting selection of single origins, which have been chosen for their bright and arresting flavour profiles.

'Coaltown creates jobs for locals struggling to find work in such a rural location'

If you're in the area, a visit to the espresso bar in the roastery is a must. Those who can't make it to Ammanford can enjoy the Coaltown experience at home via the subscription service.

Established
2014

Roaster make & size
Probat GG75 75kg,
Probat 12kg

Ammanford

85 Bay Coffee Roasters

Unit 2 Parc Tanygroes, Tanygroes, Ceredigion, SA43 2JP
baycoffeeroasters.com | 01239 814550
baycoffeeroasters

Powered by 100 per cent renewable energy, this long-established Ceredigion roastery continues to make waves in the coffee industry for its planet-friendly approach.

In 2024, Bay Coffee reached the semi finals of Roast Masters in Paris — the only roastery in the competition powered solely by renewables. It was proof that eco-friendly roasting and quality coffee can go hand in hand. A finalist place in the Sustainability Values Award category at the Wales Food and Drink Awards further cemented its eco credentials.

While sustainability is central to the Bay Coffee ethos, cup quality always leads the way. That commitment is clear in its seven years of Great Taste awards, including the highest honour: the Golden Fork.

Established
2011

Roaster make & size
Coffee Crafters
Artisan X-e 4kg x 2,
Rubasse 3kg x 2,
Aillio Bullet R1 1kg,
IKAWA Pro100

> 'While sustainability is central to the Bay Coffee ethos, cup quality always leads the way'

Whether for house blends or single origins, beans are sourced directly from ethical farms with which the team has longstanding relationships. One such partner is Hacienda Sonora in Costa Rica, where coffee is produced using hydropower.

The roastery is also a distributor of Rubasse roasters, an international leader in electric NIR (near infrared) roasting tech.

© Leandra Rieger

86 Dyfi Roastery

Not many roasters can say they bronze beans from a UNESCO biosphere. Being located at the foot of Eryri National Park, Dyfi Roastery boasts this special USP, plus a range of coffees that spark in flavour.

Unit 5, Village Workshops, Llanbrynmair, Powys, SY19 7AA

dyfiroastery.com dyfiroastery

87 Blue Monday Coffee

Need a simple way to banish the Monday blues? Brew up a flavour storm with Blue Monday's dopamine-boosting beans, roasted in Llanfihangel.

Llanfihangel-yng-Ngwynfa, Llanfyllin, Powys, SY22 5JF

bluemondaycoffee.co.uk

 bluemonday.coffee

88 Ffa Da Coffee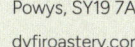

Harlech's little speciality roastery is so small-scale that beans are roasted on demand. Get your order placed via the website in time for the end-of-week roast and it'll be dispatched the following Monday. Ffa Da coffees can also be slurped from its mobile coffee van.

Llandanwg, Gwynedd, LL46 2SD

ffada.co.uk ffadacoffi

IRM Coffee Roasting Machines

Featuring air technology for **perfect roasting**.

 Air technology for efficient and consistent results every time.

 Stainless steel construction that ensures a long-lasting solution.

 Low maintenance simplifying daily operations.

 A range of roasters available for different batch amounts.

Available from **BREW-IT GROUP**
SPECIALITY COFFEE EQUIPMENT

LINK•
From **nucle**us

The ultimate sample roaster for **consistent, precise and easy roasting**.

 Roast your way from simple to complex with diverse profiles at your fingertips.

 Select your process and variety, and craft profiles all on your phone via the app.

 Roast and evaluate anytime, anywhere with the rugged, water-resistant travel case.

Available from **BREW-IT GROUP**
SPECIALITY COFFEE EQUIPMENT

BREW-IT GROUP
SPECIALITY COFFEE EQUIPMENT

Comprehensive Rental Service

All the Support You Need to Keep Serving Great Coffee.

With Brew-it Group's rental plan, we take care of everything so you can focus on making great coffee. Choose the espresso machine and grinder that suit your business, and we'll deliver and install them anywhere on the UK mainland.

Throughout your 36-month plan, you'll enjoy a full parts and labour warranty, preventative servicing every 6 months, water filter replacements, grinder burr exchanges, and even emergency call-outs at no extra cost. Every three years, you'll get a brand-new machine, keeping your setup modern and reliable. Plus, our 24/7 service line provides support whenever you need it.

Rent industry leading equipment with full support

What's included:

Espresso machine of your choice	Unlimited emergency callouts
Grinder to match your workflow	Burr + water filter replacement
Delivery + install anywhere UK mainland	24/7 service line
Regular servicing + preventative maintenance	A new machine every three years with a new agreement

For more information about how our rental service can support your business, contact us today.

Email: sales@brewitgroup.com | Tel: +44 (0)1246 454 400 | Web: www.brewitgroup.com

Menai Bridge / Y Borth

NORTH

North Wales

● Coffee shops

- 89 Riverbanc
- 90 Tabernacl
- 91 Bank Street Social
- 92 Caffeina
- 93 Corna Storr
- 94 Dudley and George's
- 95 Providero Coffeehouse – Llandudno
- 96 Eaton's
- 97 Botanical Babe Plants
- 98 Providero Coffeehouse – Llandudno Jct.
- 99 The Jester's Tower
- 100 Nonno's Coffee
- 101 Yugen Coffee House
- 102 CEIRIOS
- 103 Caffi Caban
- 104 Llofft
- 105 Caffi Tŷ Winsh Cafe
- 106 CAFE NOTOS
- 107 BRAF
- 108 The Hive

Locations are approximate

● Roasteries

- 109 Mug Run Coffee
- 110 Heartland Coffee Roasters
- 111 Poblado Coffi
- 112 Coffi Dre
- 113 Dragon Roastery

Locations are approximate

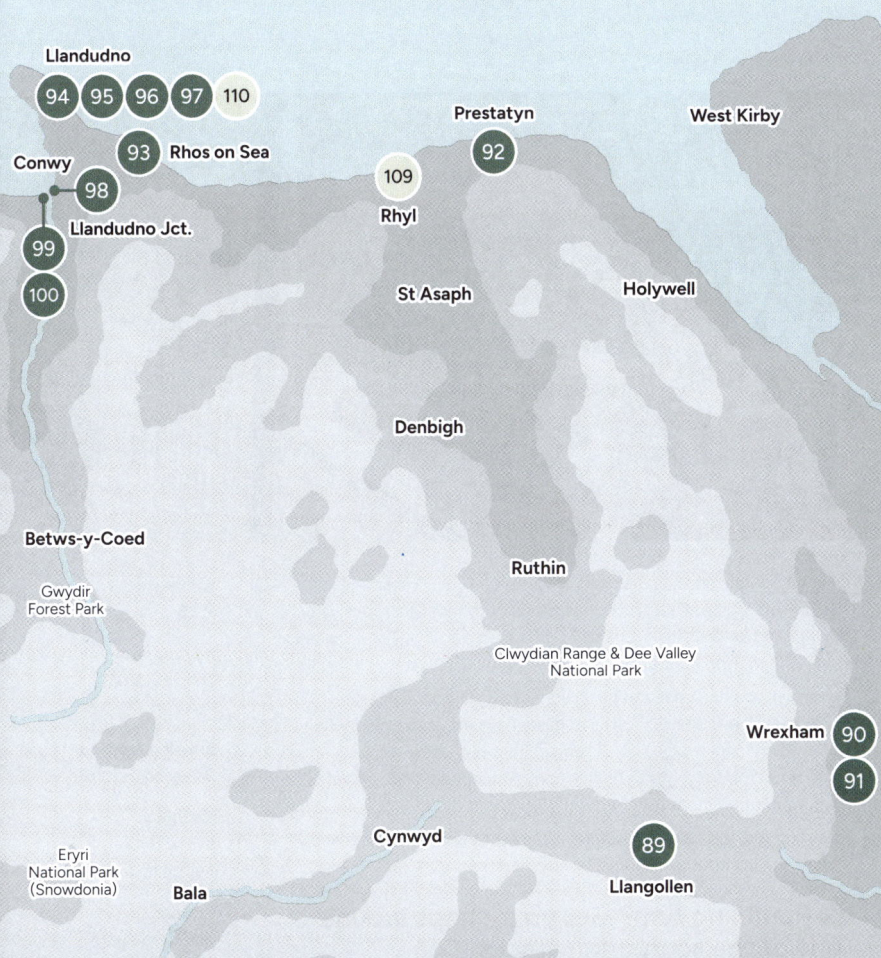

89 Riverbanc

9 Bridge Street, Llangollen, Denbighshire, LL20 8PF
riverbanc.co.uk | 01978 799903
riverbanc_llangollen

This cafe-with-rooms in the heart of Llangollen is a constant hub of activity. Its alpine-style deck is a favourite spot for outdoor adventurers who visit to sip reviving coffee after whitewater rafting on the River Dee or aqueduct canoe-touring on the Llangollen canal.

However, you don't need to be an adrenaline junkie or a guest in one of Riverbanc's seven rooms to enjoy its quality caffeine offering and sublime scenery. Locals and daytrippers also swing by for an Ozone Coffee fix and to munch on produce-led brunch plates.

Riverbanc's covered deck may be the most picturesque spot for coffee quaffing, but the inside area offers a cosy setting of reclaimed-wood tables, trailing houseplants and laidback beats.

🌱 Rumbling tum? Get your chops around one of the sourdough stacks

In a setting like this, looking after the environment is naturally front and centre and the team are constantly reassessing how they can improve their sustainability creds. Recent steps include ditching the use of single-use plastic for takeaway food and drink, increasing the use of local produce, and supporting community project Dee Valley Clean Up.

Established
2018

Key roastery
Ozone Coffee Roasters

Brewing method
Espresso

Machine
Nuova Simonelli Aurelia II

Grinder
Hey Cafe Buddy, Victoria Arduino Mythos One

Opening hours
Mon-Sun
8am-4pm

90 Tabernacl

Hope Street Church, 1-2 Hope Street, Wrexham, LL11 1BG

hopestreet.church/tabernacl

tabernaclwxm

Five years ago you wouldn't have thought the Burton Building in Wrexham town centre would be somewhere to stumble across a dynamite flat white. However, in 2022, Hope Street Church took on the building and the Tabernacl team breathed new life into this iconic venue, which had lain abandoned and crumbling for over a decade. They developed a cafe business around a trinity of principles: being ethical and sustainable, promoting community, and serving quality coffee.

These values are the lifeblood running through this church-run cafe and, to ensure everyone gets to benefit, profits go towards the community initiatives of the church, such as its toddler group and homeless outreach.

Do good and feel good: buy an extra coffee in the pay-it-forward scheme

Consistently delicious house beans are supplied by Wales' Hard Lines coffee roastery, while a guest roast is also available and regularly rotated to showcase different beans. Sample the speciality pours via espresso or batch, and bolster your order with one of the house-baked treats — the signature cookie slab is a great pairing with a fragrant batch brew.

For heartier sustenance, a refreshed food menu of waffles, salads, baps and toasties beckons.

Established
2022

Key roastery
Hard Lines

Brewing method
Espresso, batch brew

Machine
La Marzocco Linea PB

Grinder
Mahlkonig E65S GbW, Anfim Pratica

Opening hours
Tue-Sat
10am-4pm

Bank Street Social

5a Bank Street, Wrexham, LL11 1AH

bankstreetsocial.co.uk

bankstsocial

There's nothing a flat white and a natter with the Bank Street Social gang can't fix.

The Wrexham coffee shop doubles up as a community hangout where regulars are joined by passersby who've spotted the cheery chalkboard outside, sniffed the alluring waft of speciality coffee and correctly assumed this is the real deal.

The baristas tend to know returning customers' orders by heart and are dab hands at turning the house beans from Neighbourhood Coffee into slick serves. The chocolatey espresso delivers toffee and caramel sweetness that pairs perfectly with steamed milk.

Guest roasts from the likes of Wrexham Bean Co, Cracked Coffee and Hard Lines also feature and are switched up regularly.

⚫ Caffeine jitters? The (I Can't Get No) Caffeination decaf is a cracking alternative

Bank Street Social has recently garnered a new fanbase in Wrexham AFC supporters, as a result of its regular pop-up in the fan zone. A top-notch speciality brew is now considered a must while watching The Red Dragons.

Established
2017

Key roastery
Neighbourhood Coffee

Brewing method
Espresso

Machine
La Marzocco Linea PB

Grinder
Mahlkonig E80, Mahlkonig EK43, Victoria Arduino Mythos One

Opening hours
Mon-Fri
8am-3pm
Sat
9am-3pm

(92) Caffeina

28 High Street, Prestatyn, Denbighshire, LL19 9BB
caffeinacoffi.co.uk
@ caffeinacoffi

This female-owned cafe in Prestatyn is perma-busy with speciality coffee fans and those who simply like to catch up over expertly made espresso in a calming, minimalist space.

Its creative food and drink line-up and clean contemporary style bring slick city vibes to the small coastal town. As a result, it's amassed a serious following.

The cafe is often crammed (especially on Sundays when there's a run social) with discerning customers who visit to nourish body and soul with vibrant dishes and luscious brews. In addition to the espresso drinks, crafted using ALL CAPS beans, the team are known for creating colourful and leftfield concoctions such as iced blueberry matcha.

⚫ Coffee may be the main draw but the matcha is mighty fine

Indulgent bakes and freshly prepared dishes also feature on the menu. The new açai (pronounced ah sigh-ee) bowls in particular have gone bananas; try one to understand why. The bowls come in multiple varieties and pair deliciously with an iced latte or matcha. Head to the outdoor seating area to enjoy some health-giving rays while tucking in.

Established
2021

Key roastery
ALL CAPS

Brewing method
Espresso

Machine
Victoria Arduino Eagle One

Grinder
Anfim Pratica,
Mahlkonig EK43,
Victoria Arduino Mythos Two

Opening hours
Mon-Sat
8.30am-4pm
Sun
10am-3pm

93 Corna Storr

17A Rhos Road, Rhos on Sea, Conwy, LL28 4RS
cornastorr.co.uk | 01492 551516
cornastorr

This cycle-shop-meets-coffee-spot freewheels with contemporary cool and has injected Rhos on Sea with a shot of urban energy. Reflecting the cafe team's passions, the Corna Storr aesthetic combines speciality coffee with cycle and beach culture.

The Scandi style of its interiors features lots of bespoke wooden furniture, giant windows allowing the light to flood in, and a collection of vibrant houseplants. The resulting pared-back and airy vibe is a perfect backdrop for brews and fusion bites.

Beans are supplied by North Wales roastery Heartland and turned into elite coffee serves by talented baristas. Alongside espresso drinks, a batch filter from a guest roastery is always available, plus seasonal cold brew.

💡 Happy hour (any coffee and cake for a fiver) runs 3-4pm Monday to Thursday

The breakfast and lunch menus deliver elevated eats. Start the day with the likes of sour-cherry toast: tangy, buttery fruit sourdough with the option of peanut butter for extra indulgence.

Lunch takes things up another gear. Try the Mexican-inspired Baja bowl, Japanese-influenced Myoko bowl or hot-pressed sarnies – the Chilli Cham Sizzle (layers of cheddar, ham, dijon mayo and chilli jam sandwiched between Hawarden Estate sourdough) is glorious.

Established
2024

Key roastery
Heartland Coffee

Brewing method
Espresso, batch filter, cold brew

Machine
Sanremo Cafe Racer

Grinder
Mahlkonig E80 x 2,
Mahlkonig Guatemala

Opening hours
Sun-Thu
7am-4pm
Fri-Sat
7am-5pm

Dudley and George's

127 Mostyn Street, Llandudno, Conwy, LL30 2PE
dudleyandgeorges.co.uk | 01492 701689
dudleyandgeorges

There's dog friendly, then there's Dudley and George's. Yorkshire lad Jason Pinnick created the pup-centric lifestyle store as a place where dogs and their human chums can enjoy respite in equal measure.

Tongues and tails are both set wagging at the venue's in-house cafe. Two-legged visitors are treated to a firecracker of a house roast from South Wales' Big Dog Coffee and guest roasts from the likes of Little Sister Coffee Maker and Parlour Coffee.

🐾 Try the Winniepegwich, a hot egg focaccia with Juicii Hot Sauce

If you're enjoying something tasty from the array of homemade bakes, bread and scones that fill the counter each morning, it's only right to treat your furry companion too. A menu of nutritional eats for canines includes a turkey superfood salad, wild rice with wheatgrass and salmon and the new woof pizza. The latter is a one-of-a-kind creation that comes in four varieties (barkherita, sea dog, paw pollo and labradoroni). For pooches in need of a spruce up, there's also an in-house dog groomer.

Don't leave without checking out the shelves stacked with coffee beans, homewares, local produce and sustenance for friends of the four-legged variety.

Established
2020

Key roastery
Big Dog Coffee

Brewing method
Espresso,
V60, drip

Machine
Sanremo Verona

Grinder
Mahlkonig EK43,
Anfim Luna,
Eureka Zenith

Opening hours
Mon-Sun
9.30am-6pm

95 **Providero Coffeehouse** - Llandudno

112 Upper Mostyn Street, Llandudno, Conwy, LL30 2SW
providero.co.uk | 01492 338220
providerocoffee

Discover a thriving habitat of coffee culture at this roomy Llandudno coffee house – or 'Big Prov' as it's known.

Providero is cherished by both the local community and coffee geeks from further afield who visit for the next-gen brew and bean offering, diverse calendar of events (the barista workshops are raved about) and feelgood buzz.

The team strive to make speciality coffee accessible to everyone, while also staying at the top of their brew game. A Sanremo Cafe Racer was recently installed to dial up the quality even further, and every shot poured is on point.

● Weekly sessions in the upstairs Provspace Studio include yoga, dance and gong baths

Heartland Coffee Roasters supplies the trusty house blend as well as a decaf and a rotating single-origin espresso. An additional guest filter comes courtesy of leading UK roasteries and is switched up to reflect whatever palate-igniting roast the team have discovered and want to share with their coffee-enthusiast customers.

Pair your pick with something tasty from the deli menu: ciabatta and sourdough rolls are stuffed with classic fillings, while the build-your-own option appeals to fussy eaters. Don't leave without a snoop through the coffee retail section – the baristas will grind beans for your home brew method.

Established
2017

Key roastery
Heartland
Coffee Roasters

Brewing method
Espresso,
batch filter

Machine
Sanremo Cafe Racer

Grinder
Mahlkonig EK43,
Mahlkonig E80,
Mahlkonig E65S GbW,
Victoria Arduino
Mythos One Clima Pro

Opening hours
Mon-Fri
8am-4.30pm
Sat-Sun
8am-5pm

 **Eaton's**

94 Mostyn Street, Llandudno, Conwy, LL30 2SB

eatons.co.uk

eatonsllandudno

You heard it here first: there's a spanking new find on the North Wales coffee scene that's a top-quality coffee bar, farm shop and wine store in one.

Since it opened, Eaton's has brought a new coffee experience to Llandudno and it's going down a treat. Every cake on the countertop is baked in-house, the juices are freshly squeezed, the wines hand selected and the retail products chosen for their pukka provenance.

It'll come as no surprise to learn the brews are just as considered. Two seasonal coffees are roasted exclusively for the team by Big Dog Coffee (one for spring and summer sipping, the other for autumn and winter) and bronzed to complement Eaton's milk of choice: a palate-coating creamy full-fat elixir from Pentrefelin Dairy.

Think beyond ordering your usual flat white as the brew menu at Eaton's is pretty extensive, with V60, batch and drip prep methods complementing espresso. The team also dabble in trending flavour specials via homemade syrups – try the pistachio latte crafted with fresh pistachio cream.

Try the Turkish-inspired (and ultra-fragrant) cardamom long black

A commitment to supporting indie makers across the country results in an ever-changing range of quality food and drink finds on the retail shelves. Make sure your takeaway haul includes one of Eaton's own fat rascals.

Established
2025

Key roastery
Big Dog Coffee

Brewing method
Espresso, V60, batch filter, drip

Machine
Sanremo F18

Grinder
Mahlkonig E80

Opening hours
Sun-Thu
8.30am-7pm
Fri-Sat
8.30am-10pm

97 Botanical Babe Plants

66 Mostyn Street, Llandudno, Conwy, LL30 2SB
botanicalbabeplants.com | 01492 701032
botanical_babee

Pass through the trailing fronds, giant leaves and swaying palms framing the entrance to this indie plant shop and discover Tesni Boughen's oasis of speciality coffee.

Tesni designed Botanical Babe to be a tranquil space where visitors can slurp delicious coffee and – should they be tempted by the surrounding greenery – also pick up a horticultural specimen to take home.

A rotating beauty parade of single-origin espressos are roasted down the road by Heartland and includes the likes of Brazil Fazenda Picada and Honduras Armadillo Anaerobic Honey. Pourover pleasures come courtesy of a Fetco batch brew machine, which alternates between beans from Heartland and Dark Woods.

ⓘ The goat's cheese with roasted red pepper, rocket and honey on toasted sourdough is a lunchtime must

There are always at least 12 different vegan and gluten-free cakes to pair with a pour. After making their pick, customers can discover relaxing spots in which to unwind – the rattan sofa in the window is the most coveted.

Coffee goes hand in hand with culture and cultivation at this green haven: Tesni hosts regular Bloom and Bond events, including paint and sip evenings and meditation sessions.

Established
2023

Key roastery
Heartland Coffee Roasters

Brewing method
Espresso, batch filter

Machine
Sanremo F18

Grinder
Mahlkonig EK43, Mahlkonig E65S

Opening hours
Mon-Sun
8.30am-5.30pm

Providero Coffeehouse - **Llandudno Junction**

148 Conway Road, Llandudno Junction, Conwy, LL31 9DU

providero.co.uk | 01492 338220

providerocoffee

There's more to this petite Providero coffee shop ('Little Prov', to those in the know) than meets the eye.

Sure, it's the caffeine pit-stop for commuters at Llandudno Junction train station, but its homely atmosphere, walls decorated in local artwork, cosy nooks and incredible coffee offering also make it a place to relax with a brew.

The upstairs area is ideal for keyboard tapping and quiet contemplation, while downstairs emits a livelier energy as a result of its swish brew bar (check out the swanky new Sanremo gear) where baristas fix expert pours and chat with customers.

Need to decompress after a long journey? Try the sweet-as decaf

Llandudno's own speciality roastery, Heartland, supplies the goods in the duo of grinders. The house blend Landmark is reliably delicious, but adventurous coffee drinkers should scout out the single-origin option which changes every few weeks. A wildcard guest roast from the likes of Dark Arts, Dark Woods or Girls Who Grind also rotates on filter every month.

Pair the caffeinated drinks with ciabatta toasties, pastries and toothsome bakes from the light-bites menu.

Established
2014

Key roastery
Heartland
Coffee Roasters

Brewing method
Espresso,
batch filter

Machine
Sanremo D8

Grinder
Mahlkonig EK43,
Sanremo X-One

Opening hours
Mon-Sun
8am-2pm

Conwy Castle

99 · **The Jester's Tower**

Highlights at this cafe within a 700-year-old tower in Conwy's medieval quarter include Heartland brews, ancient quayside views and unexpected curios and oddities.

Castle Square, Castle Street, Conwy, LL32 8AY

thejesterstower.com thejesterstower

100 · **Nonno's Coffee**

Katie and Kenny (and doggo Reggie) are new to the speciality cafe game, having launched Nonno's at the start of 2025. However, we predict great things because of their spirited energy, slick serves and eye for beaut interiors.

22a Rose Hill Street, Conwy, LL32 8LD

 nonnos.coffee

101 · **Yugen Coffee House**

This zen-vibe cafe brings sunny antipodean coffee culture to Bangor, one cup of Allpress Espresso — and slice of avo-topped toast — at a time.

Unit 16, Menai Shopping Centre, Garth Road, Bangor, Gwynedd, LL57 1DN

yugencoffeehouse.com yugencoffeehouse

102 CEIRIOS

46 High Street, Llanberis, Caernarfon, Gwynedd, LL55 4EU

ceirioscoffee.co.uk

ceirioscoffee

Situated at the foot of Yr Wyddfa, this new small-batch roastery and micro bakery has all the makings of being a big hit with both the coffee cognoscenti and locals alike.

Ceirios is owned and run by couple Abigail and Jordan Phoenix. They produce everything in-house and share an obsessive attention to detail that helps them guarantee exceptional quality and consistency in each brew and baked good.

Check out Buddugoliaeth, the delicious Brazilian house roast

Jordan roasts a range of single-origin coffees until the clarity and depth of each batch comes through, whether it's a fruit-forward filter or sweet-caramel espresso. He then takes time transforming them into a refined menu of well-executed espresso and filter drinks, with the understanding that brewing can't be rushed if you want top-notch flavour results.

The unbeatable combination of freshly roasted coffee and just-baked treats draws in the local community — early birds know to swing by first thing if they want to nab one of the cinnamon swirls fresh from the oven.

Established
2025

Key roastery
Ceirios Coffee

Brewing method
Espresso, filter

Machine
La Marzocco Linea PB

Grinder
La Marzocco Swan, Mahlkonig EK43

Opening hours
(See Instagram for latest opening hours)

(103) Caffi Caban

Yr Hen Ysgol, Brynrefail, Caernarfon, Gwynedd, LL55 3NR
caban-cyf.org
cafficaban

Slightly suspended above the ground, glass-encased and in a semi-circular shape, Caban gives serious treehouse vibes. Bird feeders at the windows attract a variety of feathered friends and further enhance the wilderness atmos.

When the weather allows, find a perch on the deck among the foliage and bask in nature while savouring a cup of Caban's exclusive house blend, made in collaboration with local roastery Poblado Coffi. The mix of Guatemalan, Ugandan and Sumatran beans is a great base for a flat white. A guest grinder hosts single-origin beans from Poblado or Heartland, which are served as batch filter and V60.

The team craft the edibles with as much care as the coffee, and dishes are made using seasonal produce grown nearby or picked from the kitchen garden. Crowd-pleasing salad bowls crammed with organic grains and pulses are a constant, while a specials board yields delicious additional finds.

ⓘ Spread the word: Caffi Caban is now dog friendly

Caban is one of Wales' longest running social enterprises and has been at the heart of its community for over two decades. Located near Llyn Padarn and Eryri National Park, it's a popular space for local groups, laptop tappers and those refuelling after outdoor adventures. In the evening, events include gigs, markets and film screenings.

Established
2004

Key roastery
Poblado Coffi

Brewing method
Espresso, V60, batch filter

Machine
Victoria Arduino Black Eagle Gravitech

Grinder
Victoria Arduino Mythos 2, Mahlkonig EK43

Opening hours
Mon-Sun
9am–4pm

104 Llofft

Ffordd Lan y Môr, Beach Road, Y Felinheli, Gwynedd, LL56 4RQ
llofft.cymru | 01248 670554

 llofft.cymru

Llofft's story has been rooted in family and community for almost a century. The family of former owner Harry Wyn were at the helm from 1928, during which time they ran the Menai Bakery and the Sea Loft Restaurant. Fast forward and the building, overlooking the Menai Strait, has recently been transformed to a coffee shop under the care of another family: Elen ap Robert and Dylan Huws, who have a long family connection with the village.

Welsh identity is at the heart of everything the couple do, and they are keen to spread the love. Welsh is the primary language spoken in the cafe, but to help make the language more accessible to non-Welsh speakers there are encouraging prompts on the bar, e.g. *'Ga i Goffi'* (May I have a coffee?). There are also drop-in language lessons, and the website and booking system are bilingual.

🟢 Don't leave Llofft without a bag of bespoke house beans

Alongside a coffee offering that takes the form of an exclusive Brazilian-Guatemalan blend by Coffi Eryri and guest coffees from Coffi Dre, Llofft is also a bar and kitchen offering a small and eclectic menu of freshly made food crafted from local produce.

Llofft has cultivated a broad mix of customers who've joined the cafe's family – including music lovers who visit for the gigs, parents and littlies who enjoy the family-friendly vibe and those who swing by to check out the latest artwork decorating the walls.

Established
2023

Key roastery
Coffi Eryri

Brewing method
Espresso

Machine
La Spaziale S5

Grinder
Anfim Milano,
Eureka Mignon
Silenzio

Opening hours
Wed-Thu
10am-4pm
Fri-Sat
10am-10pm
Sun
10am-6pm
(seasonal opening hours - check website)

(105) Caffi Tŷ Winsh Cafe

Balaclava Road, Caernarfon, Gwynedd, LL55 1BZ
07565 944182
 tywinsh

The Caffi Tŷ Winsh building may be pretty ancient (it was built around 1850) and have oodles of historical charm but it houses a coffee offering that's most definitely 21st century.

A smart Crem espresso machine is dialled in daily to best showcase the house roast: a blend crafted by the crew at Caernarfon's Coffi Dre. The consistent result is a smooth, choc-and-nut-forward espresso.

Fans of the bespoke blend can pick up a bag to take home (ground or whole bean depending on their home brewing set-up) or explore further Coffi Dre releases such as Twthill, Porth yr Aur and Dros'r Aber.

💡 Hitting the brew menu soon: limited-edition guest blends

While grabbing a drink to-go is an option, it would be a shame to miss out on the cosy atmos of this Caernarfon cafe. It's a pleasing place for unwinding with a brew and enjoying a wholesome bite to eat. Owner Marek Sorocina and team worked hard during the cafe's recent four-month closure to refresh the space while retaining the building's character.

At the grand reopening they also unveiled a loyalty card scheme and customer wifi, making Caffi Tŷ Winsh a great find for those who want to knuckle down to a bit of keyboard bashing with a constant supply of quality caffeine on hand.

Established
2022

Key roastery
Coffi Dre

Brewing method
Espresso

Machine
Crem EX3 2GR

Grinder
Iberital MC5,
Eureka Mignon XL,
Eureka Mignon Specialita

Opening hours
Tue-Sat
10.30am-5pm

106 CAFE NOTOS

High Street, Rhosneigr, Isle of Anglesey, LL64 5UQ

cafenotos.co.uk

cafe.notos

Where better to ride the speciality wave in the coastal village of Rhosneigr than at this cute cafe? In cooler months, its warming cups of Heartland-roasted coffee and pleasing food (think stacks of pillowy pancakes and bowls of steaming ramen) provide the perfect pick-me-up. Even in chilly weather there's an opportunity to soak up the sun by eating at the ocean-wave resin countertop in the window.

The cafe's name is another nod to its maritime connection: Notos was the god of the south wind in Greek mythology, and Rhosneigr is famed for its prime watersports conditions thanks to its funnelling southerly wind.

⊘ Try one of the dishes drizzled in Notos' homemade rayu chilli oil

In warm weather, visitors can grab a table out front to feast on vibrant brunch plates and refresh themselves with iced brews, smoothies and seasonal drink specials (the cherry vanilla iced matcha is a good shout). Whatever the time of year, customers are greeted warmly by sandy-pawed pup Reggie.

Further pleasures are to be found in the fresh pastries (many plant-based), which are ideal takeaway fodder when paired with a filter brew to-go and a stomp on the beach.

Keep an eye out for regular events, including a taco and tequila night, monthly book club, burger nights and a run club.

Established
2022

Key roastery
Heartland Coffee Roasters

Brewing method
Espresso, filter

Machine
Sanremo Verona RS

Grinder
Mahlkonig EK43, Mahlkonig E80W GbS

Opening hours
Mon-Sun
7.30am-5pm

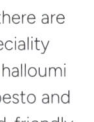

107 BRAF

There are seaside cafes – and then there are seaside cafes serving top-notch speciality brews, bouncy pancakes and Welsh halloumi and butternut-squash sarnies with pesto and hot honey on homemade bread. Grid-friendly decor and a position right on the beach make this a must-visit.

Dinas Dinlle, Caernarfon, LL54 5TW

 brafdinasdinlle

108 The Hive

What started as a horsebox cafe has grown to four cafes and a roastery in Anglesey. Owner Kristian Cuffin is the man behind Cuffed In, and he's locked down the area with his straightforward offering of house blend, house decaf and merch. Simple as.

61 Market Street, Holyhead,
Isle of Anglesey, LL65 1UN

cuffedincoffee.com cuffedincoffee

CALIFIA FARMS®

The Barista Blends Your Coffee Deserves

✓ **Subtle sweetness that perfectly complements the taste of coffee.**

✓ **Steams remarkably for creamy plant-based coffee.**

✓ **Trusted by the UK's leading specialty coffee outlets.**

Discover the Califia Farms Full Range

Plant Base Barista Blends **Flavoured Barista Blends**

For more information or to find out how to stock our products, please contact uk@califiafarms.com

NORTH ROAST-ERIES

109 Mug Run Coffee

Unit e3, Morfa Clwyd, Marsh Road, Rhyl, Denbighshire, LL18 2AF

mug-run.com | 07772 784471

@mug_run

© Ben Jones

The team at Mug Run in Denbighshire are committed to speciality coffee and the people they've encountered on their journey. This community is made up of coffee lovers from all corners of the globe, drawn together by consciously made coffee that's crafted to be accessible to everyone.

From plant to cup, the roastery gang ensure everyone in the coffee chain is treated fairly, and beans are sourced from independent farmers across the coffee-growing belt. The greens are then roasted in Norma, the crew's 10kg roaster, which ekes out nuanced flavours and honours the hard work of the growers.

The result is a range of carefully curated and diverse roasts to satisfy both retail and wholesale customers. The Shed Blend showcases a harmonious balance of flavours and delivers chocolatey and fruity notes with a sweet finish. As much care is taken when selecting decaf as fully caffeinated coffees, and the beans are decaffeinated using the natural sparkling water method.

'The result is a range of carefully curated and diverse roasts'

The team are continuously upping their reuse and recycle game, and source supplies locally to keep the miles and carbon footprint low. They also collaborate with other indies and makers in their area.

Delve further into the Mug Run cosmos by setting up a subscription, booking onto a coffee course, or catching the crew at markets and coffee festivals.

Established
2013

Roaster make & size
Bespoke 10kg

Heartland Coffee Roasters

Unit 6 Cwrt Roger Mostyn, Builder Street, Llandudno, LL30 1DS
heartland.coffee | 01492 878757
heartland.coffee

The Heartland crew care deeply about elevating the coffee experience for those at the beginning and the end of the speciality journey: the farmers and the coffee sippers.

Over the past year, the team have been busy working on a major brand revamp while also unveiling some unique coffees from renowned producers like CGLE. Look out for the Colombia XO and an incredible yeast-inoculated pink bourbon from Quebraditas.

They've also continued to build on their close relationship with Café Granja La Esperanza in Colombia, whose expertise lies in the horticultural side of coffee, and have refined some innovative cultivars which are now exclusive to the farm. The roasters are also satisfying their customers' increased appetite for single origins. To please fans of more classic coffees, the crew also source beans from Cargo in Brazil, which delivers relationship coffees from single-family farms.

'Look out for the incredible yeast-inoculated pink bourbon'

In a bid to give more coffee lovers the chance to sip amid the buzz of the roastery, the in-house brew bar and adjoining hangout is about to be made even bigger. Visit to taste the Great Taste award-winning Landmark blend and the Swiss Water decaf.

Established
2005

Roaster make & size
Coffee-Tech Ghibli 45kg
Coffee-Tech Ghibli 15kg

111 Poblado Coffi

Unit 1, Y Barics, Nantlle, Caernarfon, Gwynedd, LL54 6BD
pobladocoffi.co.uk | 01286 882555
poblado_coffi

Visiting Eryri or the beautiful North Wales coast? Schedule in a detour to this coffee roastery housed in a former quarrymen's barracks.

In summer, the barracks' door is flung open, and locals and visiting caffeine fiends congregate in the courtyard for alfresco coffee and cake. While the summer weekend sessions are the busiest, owner Steffan Huws and his team are happy to welcome passersby for a chat and a brew on any day of the week – if the door's open, the coffee machine's on. The fleet of foot can get a further wellbeing fix by joining the Poblado Plodders, a running community that hits the road on Saturday mornings.

Exciting plans are brewing for Steffan and crew, who are currently renovating an old chapel. When it's complete, it will house a second roaster, a visitor and training centre, a cafe and an events venue.

Established
2013

Roaster make & size
Giesen 15kg

'Exciting plans are brewing for Steffan and crew, who are currently renovating an old chapel'

At the heart of the current set-up is a 15kg Giesen, which roasts Poblado's curated collection of blends and single origins. Steffan has forged long-term relationships with growers and selects lots from across the globe for their eco credentials.

New to Poblado? Sign up for an Explore Bundle or Variety Pack subscription, which is the easiest way to sample the range.

112 Coffi Dre

Caernarfon, Gwynedd

coffidre.cymru

@ coffidre

In summer 2021, Ceurwyn Humphreys teamed up with close pal Haydn Riley-Walsh to launch Coffi Dre.

The roastery is named after the town in which it resides (Coffi Dre roughly translates into English as 'Caernarfon Coffee'), and the duo at the helm channel a fierce passion for Welsh culture, language and community into every batch of beans they roast.

Ceurwyn and Haydn select top-quality beans from farms across the coffee-growing belt, bronzing them in a Pacrone or Besca roaster to unleash their distinctive flavours. Highlights from the range include Twthill (a lively Indian blend that takes its name from a historic hill overlooking Caernarfon) and Porth yr Aur (a smooth Colombian coffee named after the town's 13th-century golden gate). Beans are packaged in bags featuring artwork reflecting the landscape, stories and creativity of North Wales.

'Our goal is to celebrate Caernarfon through speciality coffee'

The Coffi Dre crew roast their beans in a converted shipping container so space is at a premium. However, demand is so high that they've just added a 10kg Besca to the roasting tech line-up. Ceu and Haydn also pitch up at events and serve quality brews from their converted horsebox.

'We're always learning and improving,' says Ceu. *'From eco-friendly packaging to supporting the community, our goal is to celebrate Caernarfon through amazing speciality coffee.'*

Established
2021

Roaster make & size
Pacrone5 5kg
Besca 10kg

(113) **Dragon Roastery**

This roastery (the first in Anglesey) has grown a cult following on the island for its punchy, full-flavoured beans. Look out for the roastery's cherry-red horsebox-turned-cafe and roadtest them for yourself.

Stryd Pendref, Newborough, Anglesey, LL61 6TB
dragonroastery.co.uk 🅾 dragonroastery

Notes

Somewhere to keep a record of exceptional beans and brews you've discovered on your coffee adventures

Notes

The UK's best coffee – in your pocket!

Get the NEW app

Have *Indy Coffee Guide London* at your fingertips, wherever you go.

- Interactive maps
- Know where's good nearby
- Save your faves
- Get all the deets on each cafe
- Be first to know about new cafes + events

UK-wide app coming soon

Download now

indycoffee.guide/app

INDEX

A

Alex Gooch Shops	42
Angel Bakery, The	36

B

Baffle Haus	37
Bank Street Social	118
Baravin	102
Basekamp	65
Bay Coffee Roasters	108
Bay Coffee Roasters Cafe	95
Bean & Bread	34
Beat Bakehouse	58
Blue Monday Coffee	109
Blŵm	40
Boo's Kitchen	73
Booths by the Bridge	63
Botanical Babe Plants	124
BRAF	132
Brickworks Coffee	38

C

CAFE NOTOS	131
Caffeina	119
Caffi Caban	128
Caffi Castell Harlech	103
Caffi Siop Plas	103
Caffi Tŷ Winsh Cafe	130
CannaDeli	50
CEIRIOS	127
Clwb Coffi	61
Coaltown Coffee Roasters	107
Coaltown Espresso Bar	93
Coffi a Bara	100
Coffi Dre	139
Coffi Lab	37
Coffiology	37
Corna Storr	120
Corner Coffee – Cardiff	46
Corner Coffee – Porthcawl	57
Crafty Smuggler Coffee	67
Cribyn Coffee Company	106
Crwst	100

D

Diod	96
Donald's Coffee & Pies – Quay Street	47
Donald's Coffee & Pies – Radyr	39
Double Trouble Coffee Roasters	81
Dragon Roastery	140
Duck & Dough	68
Dudley and George's	121
Dugout Cafébar, The	35
Dyfi Roastery	109

E

Eaton's	123

F

Ffa Da Coffee	109
Fikamumbles	73

G

Georgie Porgies	88
Get the Boys a Lift	97
Gourmet Pig, The	98
Greenhouse Cafe & Kitchen	86
Ground Plant Based Coffee	70
Gwesty Cymru	101

H

Hard Lines – roastery	79
Hard Lines – cafe	50
Haystack Cafe – Merthyr Tydfil	62
Heartland Coffee Roasters	137
Hive, The	132
HMY	96
Humble Coffi	92
Hyde Out, The	60

J

Jester's Tower, The	126

K

KIN+ILK	50
Kontext Coffee Company	81

L

Latte-Da	88
Life of Reilly Coffee Co.	54
Lle Tarw	75
Llofft	129

M

Mec Coffee	42
Microlot by Mumbles Coffee	72
Milkwood	50
Monty's	64
Motley Pie	73
Mug Run Coffee	136
Mumbles Coffee	71

N

Narrative Coffee	87
Nonno's Coffee	126
Nook & Noble	99

O

Oat & Bean	43
Outside The Box	74

P

Pitchfork & Provision	94
Poblado Coffi	138
Providero Coffeehouse – Llandudno	122
Providero Coffeehouse – Llandudno Jct.	125

Q

Quantum Coffee Roasters – Cardiff	44
Quantum Coffee Roasters – Cardiff Bay	51

R

Rate of Rise Coffee	78
Rhostio Coffee Roasters	41
Riverbanc	116

Page no

S

Saint Hugo	70
Scaredy Cats Cafe Bar	45
Scout Coffee Roasters	81
Shire Coffee at HWYL	89
Shire Coffee at The Bookshop	90
Sibling	42
Sloth Coffee Co.	69
Sparrow Coffee House	42
Square Peg Coffee House	70
Steel Town Coffee Company	62
Stomping Ground	55
Storm in a Teacup Coffeehouse	66

T

Tabernacl	117
T-Boi Coffee	91
Two Islands	103

U

Uncommon Ground – Cathedral Road	49
Uncommon Ground Coffee Roastery	48

W

Welsh Coffee Co. – cafe	56
Welsh Coffee Co. – roastery	80
Whocult Coffee + Donuts	59

Y

Yugen Coffee House	126

FOR BREW FRE &BEA GEEK

With the full collection of *Indy Coffee Guides* to hand, you'll always know where to find the best speciality coffee in the UK.

Shop the full range, including the app and guides for: London; the South of England; North, Midlands and East; and Scotland at

indycoffee.guide